THE COMMONSENSE
SCOTS
COOKERY BOOK

THE COMMONSENSE SCOTS COOKERY BOOK

Gordon Hay

ANGUS & ROBERTSON · PUBLISHERS

Angus & Robertson Publishers
Brighton • Sydney • Melbourne • Singapore • Manila

First published by Angus & Robertson (UK) Ltd,
16 Ship Street, Brighton, Sussex BN1 1AD, in 1978

Copyright © Gordon Hay and Wink Ltd 1978

ISBN 0 207 95797 5

Printed in Great Britain by
Hazell Watson & Viney Ltd, Aylesbury, Bucks

CONTENTS

To Ann and Nigel
but especially
to Catherine,
who has tolerated me in her
kitchen for thirty-nine years.
I have often left it in a 'gae sotter'.

Oh Siccan a sottar was a' body in,
Five mile awa' ye could hear the din;
Nae wonder the very coo' started to grin
At the muckin' o' Geordie's byre.

(Traditional bothy ballad)

Note in Reply to an Invitation

Sir,
Yours this moment I unseal,
And faith I'm gay and hearty!
To tell the truth, and shame the deil,
I am as fu' as Bartie;
But Foorsday, sir, my promise leal,
Expect me o' your partie,
If on a beastie I can speel,
Or hurl in a cartie.
Yours,
Robert Burns
Machlin, Monday night, 10 o'clock

ACKNOWLEDGEMENTS

Among the many people who have helped me in gathering material for this book I must first thank Rosemary Wadey. Rosemary, a freelance home economist and writer, tested and examined the bulk of the recipes under normal domestic conditions in her country cottage kitchen. A number of recipes were also tested by Ray Grainge.

William George Cowie, who was at school with me in Buckie, is an authority on lowland Scots dialect and spent endless time checking the manuscript.

The following have helped me in various ways: His Grace the Duke of Atholl; Richard Baker, BSc; Baxters of Fochabers; Lt. Col. T. O. Cowan, BSc; Drambuie; Gordon & McPhail, Elgin; Hamlyn Angus Milling Co, Kirriemuir (who supplied the oatmeal); Harrods Ltd, London; Herring Industry Board, Edinburgh; Isle of Arran Canneries; the Mitchell Library, Glasgow; the Central Library, Aberdeen; Pitshanger Library, Ealing; Catherine Lister; Tory Research Station, Aberdeen; Captain G. G. Wilson, OBE; W. G. Young—and a great many friends and acquaintances who have given me information, entertained me and stimulated my mind and my appetite.

I have consulted a number of publications, notably *The Cook and Housewife's Manual* (1826) by Margaret Dods (there are several of her recipes in *The Commonsense Scots Cookery Book*); also *The Scots Kitchen* (Blackie & Sons, 1929) by Marian McNeill.

The tartans shown in the illustrations in this book were supplied by Kinloch Anderson Ltd, Edinburgh, as follows: Dress Gordon (illustrations nos. 2 and 18); Red Innes (14, top); Dress McDuff (14, bottom); The Lord of the Isles (cover); McKenzie (Seaforth Highlanders) (12, right); McLaren (3 and 12, left); Dress McPherson (1); McPherson Red (15, right); Ogilvie of Airlie (17, centre); Hunting Sinclair (4); Sinclair Red (15, left); Dress Stewart (17, bottom); Royal Stewart (10 and 16); Strathearn (17, top).

Note: All references to Scots county names in this book are based on the old boundaries before their rearrangement in 1975.

ILLUSTRATIONS

INTRODUCTION

At a time when every month seems to see the publication of a new cookery book, why should we produce another one — and a Scots one at that?

Scotland is in a state of transition. As a result of a boosted economy primed by the discovery of offshore oil, life has changed for ever. In addition, there has been an influx of so-called 'settlers' from the congested south in search of tranquillity in one of the world's few remaining peaceful and uncrowded areas. An over-rapid injection of economic prosperity so often results in the decline, or entire elimination, of age-old country customs. If this were to occur in rural Scotland, not only the antiquarians would regret it. While some adjustment must be made to a new environment, this should be done without jettisoning the values of the past. It is with this factor very much in the forefront of my mind that this book was written.

I have collected and examined a great many old recipes, and have had them brought up to date, adapting instructions like 'cook on a dying fire' to suit present cooking conditions. At the same time, I have left out some traditional dishes that involve methods thoroughly impracticable for most people — so I will not recommend that you bury your fresh-caught haddocks under turf before drying them in the sun, nor advise you to get your sheep's head singed by the village blacksmith. This is not a search into old Scottish eating habits but a collection of recipes illustrating the best of food and drink in Scotland.

Scots cookery was, of course, always based primarily on the produce of the land and sea — before the freedom of travel, most eating habits were necessarily local. The traditional 'cottar' or cottage cooking exemplifies this, dictated by a low income and the availability of milk, oatmeal, potatoes, a few other vegetables and, in coastal areas, an abundance of fish. Distinct from this was the 'big hoose' cookery enjoyed by the gentry in their big houses. These households, of lairds, ministers, doctors and lawyers, would have a more sophisticated approach, influenced by the south and imbued with a culture from the 'Auld Alliance' with France. ('Gigot', 'ashet' and 'tassie' are three good Scots words lifted bodily from the French.) This resulted in high standards of cookery and deportment in many kitchens, standards learnt by the village girls who worked in the kitchens, and often applied by them when they returned to their own homes.

The sad thing today is that many hotels catering for the considerable tourist industry in Scotland generally fail to make up their menus from this cookery heritage. If you are an unfortunate victim of such a circumstance, then enjoy your own Scots cookery at home!

WEIGHTS AND MEASURES

Quantities in this book are given in metric and imperial. It is important to note that they are only approximately equivalent. The metric measurement for weight is based here on the 25-gramme unit being equivalent to 1 ounce — as there are actually 28.35 grammes in 1 ounce, metric amounts in the recipes are slightly smaller than imperial. One system only should be used consistently, otherwise the proportions will be wrong.

Measurements are also given in teaspoons and tablespoons, and always refer to a level spoonful. It should be noted that the British teaspoon and tablespoon are both slightly larger than their American counterpart: 1 UK teaspoon=1.20 US teaspoon; 1 UK tablespoon=1.25 US tablespoon.

Generally speaking, a little extra here or there does little or no harm to a recipe, except in baking, where for the best results every care should be taken to be accurate.

Note: All recipes are for 4, unless otherwise stated.

SOUPS

'Soup has been termed the vestibule to the banquet. We call it the only true foundation to the principal repast of the day.'
Mrs Margaret Dods

Margaret Dods's 1826 recipe for 'skink', an old Scottish soup, begins: 'Take two legs of beef, put them on with two gallons of water, let them boil for six hours. . . .' That must have been the kind of thing to deter later potential soup-makers. But today, anyone can make good soup, provided that he or she is pre-pared to start off by making good stock. Several recipes for stock are given here; and occasionally a short cut can be taken by using instant stock powder or cubes.

Do not hesitate to add to or deduct from the quantities given in the recipes for vegetables, barley and rice. Some people like their soup very thick, and make enough for two days. 'Second day's broth' is always popular in a Scottish home. If you have a deep freeze, use it for your soups — they will keep beautifully. Remember that milk does not freeze well, so if the recipe includes milk, add it after the soup has thawed out. If you have surplus stock, freeze that too, and add the other ingredients for the soup when you are ready.

There is an old story that illustrates a traditional Scots attitude towards soup-making. Queen Victoria spent a great deal of time at Balmoral Castle after Prince Albert died, and she often visited the estate workers' cottages. On one visit, an old Highland lady ventured to offer Her Majesty a plate of the Scotch broth which was cooking on the fire. The Queen accepted, was delighted with it, and inquired, 'What is this soup called?' 'Intilt soup,' was the reply. 'Why "intilt" soup?' asked the Queen. Came the answer, 'A' thing gaes intilt' (Everything goes into it).

STOCK-MAKING

Brown Stock

400 g (1 lb) marrow bones or
  cooked bones or knuckle of
  veal
200–400 g (½–1 lb) shin of beef
  (optional)
2.5 litres (5 pints) water
Bouquet garni (see p. 3)
2 carrots, peeled and sliced
1–2 onions, peeled and chopped
1–2 sticks celery, chopped
Salt

Chop the bones, cube the meat, and to give a good colour brown in a hot oven before using. Place all the ingredients in a large pan, bring to the boil, skim and remove any fat. Cover and simmer for 4–6 hours. Strain and cool. Skim off any more fat. Keep in the refrigerator and use within 2–4 days.

White Stock

800 g (2 lb) knuckle of veal or
veal and mutton bones
2 litres (4 pints) water
½ lemon (optional)
1–2 onions, peeled and chopped
1–2 carrots, peeled and sliced
Bouquet garni (see p. 3)
Salt

Put the bones into a large pan with all the other ingredients and bring to the boil. Remove scum, cover and simmer for 4–5 hours. Strain, cool and remove fat. Keep in the refrigerator and use within 2–4 days.

Poultry or Game Stock

Make in the same way as brown stock, using the raw or cooked carcass and giblets of any poultry or game without browning in the oven. Simmer for 3–4 hours. Keep in the refrigerator and use within 2–4 days.

Note: If using instant stock cubes or powder for convenience, try beef for brown stock and chicken for white stock. Take care when adding seasonings, for stock cubes tend to be salty. It is advisable to strain dissolved stock through muslin to remove the herbs and other pieces floating in it as they may spoil the appearance of some soups.

Fish Stock

1 cod's head or fish trimmings
Cold water
Salt
Bouquet garni (see below)
1–2 onions, peeled and sliced
2 carrots, peeled and sliced

Clean and wash the cod's head or trimmings and place in a pan. Cover with water and add other ingredients. Bring to the boil, skim, cover and simmer for 40 minutes. Strain, keep in the refrigerator, and use within 2–4 days.

BOUQUET GARNI

These can be bought in muslin bags or made up as required using fresh or dried herbs.

Fresh Bouquet Garni

1 bayleaf
2 sprigs of parsley
1 sprig of thyme
Few peppercorns
1 blade of mace

Tie all together in a small square of muslin and use at once.

Dried Bouquet Garni

1 bayleaf
6 peppercorns
1 blade of mace
2 cloves
Pinch of dried mixed herbs
Pinch of dried parsley

Tie all together in a small square of muslin. Make several at a time and store in an airtight container.

CHICKEN BROTH

1 litre (2 pints) good chicken
    stock
40 g (1½ oz) long-grain rice
1 onion, peeled and finely
    chopped
1 leek, cleaned and chopped
Salt and pepper
125 ml (¼ pint) milk (optional)
1 tablespoon chopped parsley

Place stock in a pan and bring to the boil. Add rice, onion, and the white part of the leek, and season well. Simmer gently for 30 minutes, then add the green part of the leek and continue to simmer for 15 minutes. Add the milk, if used, adjust seasonings, stir in parsley and serve. Serves 5–6.

Note: Barley or small macaroni can be used instead of rice.

GIBLET SOUP

400 g (1 lb) giblets
2 onions, peeled and chopped
2 large sticks celery, chopped
2 carrots, peeled and chopped
Salt and pepper
1.5 litres (3 pints) water
1 bayleaf
40 g (1½ oz) rice
2 large carrots, peeled and grated
Chopped parsley

Wash giblets thoroughly then put in a pan with the onions, celery, carrots, seasoning, water and bayleaf. Bring to the boil, skim, then cover and simmer gently for about 2 hours. Strain and return soup to the pan with the rice, grated carrot and some of the finely chopped giblet meat. Some of the cooked vegetables can also be liquidized or sieved and added to the soup. Simmer for a further 15–20 minutes, adjust seasonings and serve sprinkled with parsley. Serves 6–8.

COCK-A-LEEKIE

1–1.5 kg (2½–3½ lb) oven-ready boiling fowl
1.5–2 litres (3–4 pints) stock or water
4 leeks, cleaned and sliced
Salt and black pepper
Bouquet garni (see p. 3)
1 prune (soaked overnight) per portion

Place the trussed bird in a large pan with the stock or water, leeks, seasoning and bouquet garni. Bring to the boil, remove scum, cover and simmer gently for 2½–3 hours till almost tender. Add prunes and continue for a further 30 minutes. Remove bird, serve it separately but first chop a little of the meat and return to the soup. Adjust seasonings and serve. Serves 6–8.

Note: Serve the chicken cold with salad or with a good sauce. Cold boiled chicken has a flavour quite distinct from roast chicken, and is paler in colour.

The inclusion of prunes served one to each plate of soup is not universal and is controversial (raisins were used at one time). The comment of the 'Ettrick Shepherd', James Hogg, may be acceptable to some: 'The man was an atheist that first polluted it with prunes.'

FEATHER FOWLIE

1–1.5 kg (2½–3½ lb) boiling fowl or 4 chicken portions
Pieces of leftover ham or bacon
Bouquet garni (see p. 3)
2 sticks celery, chopped
1 large onion, chopped
Salt and pepper
1 litre (2 pints) water
1 tablespoon chopped parsley
2 egg yolks
2–4 tablespoons single (light) cream

Wash the fowl well and place in a large pan with the ham or bacon, bouquet garni, celery, onion, seasonings and water. Bring to the boil, remove scum, cover and simmer gently for 1½–2 hours till tender. Strain soup and remove any grease with a spoon. Add parsley and the finely chopped meat from one portion of chicken and bring to the boil. Remove from heat and whisk in egg yolks blended with a little of the soup and the cream. Adjust seasonings, reheat without boiling and serve. Serves 4–6.

BAWD BREE (Hare Soup)

1 hare, cut into portions
Hare's blood
50 g (2 oz) streaky bacon, chopped
2 onions, peeled and chopped
40 g (1½ oz) dripping
3.5 litres (6–7 pints) water
Salt and pepper
½ turnip, peeled and chopped
2 carrots, peeled and chopped
2 sticks celery, chopped
Bouquet garni (see p. 3)
50 g (2 oz) fine oatmeal or flour
1–2 tablespoons redcurrant or
    rowan jelly
125 ml (¼ pint) port

Keep the blood carefully. Fry bacon and onions in the dripping till brown then add hare, water and seasonings. Bring to the boil, skim, cover and simmer for 2 hours. Add vegetables and bouquet garni and simmer for 2 hours longer. Strain. Finely chop some of the hare meat (use the best parts for Jugged Hare or other dishes, see p. 66) and return to the soup with the oatmeal or flour blended in a little water. Bring to the boil and simmer for 30 minutes. Stir in jelly, blood and port, adjust seasonings and reheat without boiling. Serves 12–16, depending on the size of the hare.

KIDNEY SOUP (WITH DUMPLINGS)

200 g (½ lb) ox kidney, skinned,
    cored and chopped
3 tablespoons seasoned flour
1 large onion, peeled and finely
    chopped
40 g (1½ oz) dripping or butter
1 litre (2 pints) brown stock
Bouquet garni (see p. 3)
Salt and pepper
Gravy browning
Dumplings (see below)

Toss kidney in some of the seasoned flour, then fry with the onion in dripping or butter for about 5 minutes till beginning to brown. Add stock and bouquet garni and bring to the boil. Cover and simmer for about 1½ hours till tender. Liquidize or sieve if a smooth soup is preferred. Blend 2 tablespoons of seasoned flour with a little water then add the same amount of hot soup. Gradually whisk back into the soup and bring to the boil. Adjust seasoning and add a little gravy browning if necessary. Serve with or without dumplings.

Dumplings

100 g (4 oz) self-raising flour
50 g (2 oz) shredded or chopped
    suet
Salt and pepper
½ teaspoon mixed herbs (optional)
½ small onion, finely grated
    (optional)
Cold water
A little flour

Mix the flour, suet, salt and pepper, and herbs and onion if used, with sufficient cold water to give an elastic dough. Form into 16 balls, using a little flour to prevent sticking, and add to the soup or stew for 15–20 minutes before serving. Serves 4–8.

SCOTCH BROTH

600 g (1½ lb) neck of mutton or
  lamb
2 litres (4 pints) water
100 g (4 oz) pearl barley (soaked
  overnight)
100 g (4 oz) dried peas (soaked
  overnight)
Salt and pepper
1–2 leeks, cleaned and chopped
1 onion, peeled and chopped
1 medium turnip, peeled and
  chopped
3 large carrots, peeled and
  chopped
¼ small cabbage (optional)
1 tablespoon chopped parsley

Trim off excess fat and cut meat into pieces. Place in a large pan with the water, barley, peas and plenty of salt and pepper. Bring to the boil and skim. Add leeks, onion, turnip and carrots, and simmer for about 3 hours. Add finely shredded cabbage if required, adjust seasonings and simmer for a further 30–45 minutes. Remove any fat on the surface with a spoon, add parsley and serve hot. Traditionally the meat is served with a little of the broth and the remaining broth is served separately. Serves 6–8.

Note: Shin of beef and a marrow bone can be used in place of mutton for a change.

OXTAIL SOUP

1 oxtail, jointed
25 g (1 oz) dripping or butter
2 onions, peeled and chopped
2 carrots, peeled and sliced
2 sticks celery, chopped
2 litres (4 pints) brown stock
25 g (1 oz) lean bacon or ham,
  chopped
Bouquet garni (see p. 3)
Salt and pepper
3 tablespoons flour
4–6 tablespoons port, sherry or
  water
1 tablespoon lemon juice

Wash and dry oxtail and trim off excess fat. Brown in the dripping or butter with the vegetables then add stock till just covered. Add ham, bouquet garni and seasonings, bring to the boil, cover and simmer gently for 3–4 hours or till tender. Skim off fat when necessary during cooking. If possible cool overnight and remove solid layer of fat. Reheat, then strain soup. Remove meat from the bones, chop and add to the liquor. Blend flour with a little port, sherry or water and whisk gradually into the soup. Bring to the boil for 3 minutes. Add lemon juice and adjust seasoning before serving. Serves 6–10.

Note: Dumplings (see recipe on p. 5) can be added if required, and the soup can be served with the vegetables unstrained and the meat left on the bone.

Top: Soups: Lentil (p. 9), Oatmeal Vegetable (p. 10) and Cock-a-Leekie (p. 4) with Glasgow Floury Baps (p. 89).

Bottom: Skipper's Pie (p. 28), Potted Herrings (p. 17) and Trout with Almonds (p. 27), with fresh herrings.

HOTCHPOTCH

This is a delicious hearty broth made from young summer vegetables. Use any vegetables as long as they are young and fresh.

1-1.25 kg (2–3 lb) neck of mutton or lamb
3 litres (5–6 pints) water
Salt and pepper
300 g (12 oz) shelled broad beans
700 g (1¾ lb) shelled peas
12 spring onions, trimmed
4 young turnips, peeled and chopped
4 young carrots, peeled and chopped
1 small cauliflower
1 small lettuce
2–3 tablespoons chopped parsley

Cut up meat and place in a large pan with the water and seasonings. Bring to the boil and skim. Add beans, onions, turnips, carrots and half the peas. Cover and simmer for 3–4 hours. Skim off any fat then add sprigs of cauliflower, lettuce and remaining peas. Simmer for a further 30 minutes. Adjust seasonings, add parsley and serve. Serves 10–12.

VENISON SOUP

50 g (2 oz) dripping
200 g (½ lb) lentils
2 onions, peeled and chopped
1 small turnip, peeled and chopped
2 large carrots, peeled and chopped
2 litres (4 pints) venison stock (see below)
Salt and pepper
Double (heavy) cream for garnish

Melt dripping in a pan and sauté lentils and vegetables for 3–4 minutes. Add stock, salt and pepper and bring to the boil. Skim thoroughly then cover pan and simmer gently for 2–3 hours. Strain through a hair sieve for a clear soup, or liquidize if preferred. Return to the pan, reheat, adjust seasonings, and finely chop any pickings of venison from the bones and add to the soup. Serve with a spoonful of cream on top with fried bread croûtons, if liked. Serves 8–10.

Note: To make venison stock place any raw or cooked venison bones and trimmings and — if possible — the hock in a large pan with an onion. Cover with water, bring to the boil, skim and simmer very gently in a covered pan for 6–8 hours. Strain and use. Remove any pickings of meat from the bones and add to the soup.

Poached Salmon (p. 25) with new potatoes, salad, Oatcakes (p. 79) and mayonnaise.

HOUGH SOUP

200 g (½ lb) hough or shin of beef
1 litre (2 pints) water
1 large onion, peeled and sliced
25 g (1 oz) dripping or butter
Salt and pepper
1 bayleaf
Few black peppercorns
25 g (1 oz) flour, cornflour (corn-starch) or sago

Cut the meat into small cubes and soak in the cold water for 30 minutes. Fry onion in dripping or butter till golden brown; then pour off any excess fat. Add meat and water, salt and pepper, bayleaf and pepper-corns and bring to the boil. Skim, cover and simmer for 2–3 hours. Strain soup and return to a clean pan. Blend chosen thickening with a little cold water and whisk into the soup. Bring to the boil and simmer for 10 minutes. Adjust seasonings, chop meat finely and return to the pan. Reheat for 5 minutes before serving. Serves 4–6.

SKINK SOUP

600–800 g (1½–2 lb) shin or leg of beef
1 marrow bone
Salt and pepper
1 bayleaf
2 litres (4 pints) water
600 g (1½ lb) mixed turnips, parsnips and onions, peeled and chopped
4–6 sticks celery, chopped
½ small cabbage, finely shredded

Place the meat and bone in a large pan with salt, pepper and bayleaf and add the water. Bring to the boil, skim and cover. Simmer slowly for 3–4 hours till meat is tender. Strain, return to the pan and remove any fat. Cut meat into neat cubes and keep aside. Add the vegetables and simmer for 45–60 minutes. Return meat to the pan, adjust seasonings and simmer for 10 minutes before serving. Serves 8–10.

LEEK AND POTATO POTAGE

2 rashers streaky bacon
25 g (1 oz) butter
2 large leeks, cleaned and sliced
400 g (1 lb) potatoes, peeled and sliced
1 clove garlic, crushed (optional)
500 ml (1 pint) white stock
Salt and pepper
Approx 200 ml (¼–½ pint) milk
2 tablespoons chopped parsley
75 g (3 oz) finely grated cheese

Derind and chop the bacon and fry it in butter till lightly brown, then add leeks, potatoes, and crushed garlic if used, and continue frying for 5 minutes. Stir in stock and seasonings and simmer, covered, for 30–40 minutes till tender. Add enough milk to give the required consistency, check seasonings and reheat. Stir in parsley and serve with the cheese handed separately. Serves 4–6.

Note: Liquidize or sieve, if preferred.

LENTIL SOUP

100 g (4 oz) lentils (see note
  below)
25 g (1 oz) dripping
2 carrots, peeled and diced
1 clove garlic, crushed (optional)
1 small turnip or swede, peeled
  and diced
1 large onion, peeled and diced
1 litre (2 pints) water
1 hock or knuckle of bacon or a
  ham bone (preferably smoked)
Salt and pepper
1 potato, peeled and chopped

Soak lentils overnight in cold water. Melt dripping in a pan and sauté carrots, garlic, turnip or swede, and onion for 5 minutes. Add lentils, water and ham bone. Bring to the boil, cover and simmer gently for about 2 hours. Season well, add potato and more boiling water if necessary and continue for a further 30–60 minutes. Remove bone, add a little chopped ham and serve piping hot with croûtons. Serves 6.

Note: To make a thicker soup increase or even double the quantity of lentils but stir regularly while cooking to avoid burning. I like it really thick with plenty of white pepper. Make pea soup by substituting 150 g (6 oz) split peas for the lentils, and adding a little green colouring if necessary. Bean soup can be made using 150 g (6 oz) haricot beans which have been soaked overnight in water.

ONION SOUP

This old Scottish recipe is for a white soup, unlike the traditional brown French onion soup.

25 g (1 oz) butter or margarine
400 g (1 lb) onions, peeled and
  finely chopped
1–2 sticks celery, finely chopped
750 ml (1½ pints) white stock
1 blade of mace
1 bayleaf
Salt and pepper
25 g (1 oz) flour
125 ml (¼ pint) milk
Chopped parsley

Melt the butter or margarine in a pan and sauté onions and celery for 5 minutes without colouring. Add stock, mace, bayleaf and seasonings and bring to the boil. Cover and simmer for ¾–1 hour till tender. Remove bayleaf and mace. Blend flour carefully with the milk and whisk gradually into the soup. Return to the boil, stirring all the time. Adjust seasonings and simmer for 5 minutes before serving sprinkled with parsley. Serves 4–6.

Note: If a smooth soup is preferred it may be liquidized or sieved. A little celery salt can be used in place of the celery and shallots can be used in place of the onions.

COURT BOUILLON

This is used to enhance the flavour when poaching fish such as salmon, sea and freshwater trout and fish steaks, or large pieces of fish such as turbot and halibut.

1 litre (2 pints) water (or dry white wine and water mixed)
1 carrot, peeled and sliced
1 small onion, peeled and sliced
1 stick celery, sliced
1 tablespoon vinegar or lemon juice
Few sprigs of parsley
½–1 bayleaf
4 peppercorns
1–2 teaspoons salt

Place all the ingredients in a pan, bring to the boil, cover and simmer for about 30 minutes. Allow to cool and use either as it is or strained if preferred. The amount of water used depends on the size of fish to be cooked.

OATMEAL VEGETABLE SOUP

50 g (2 oz) dripping or butter
1 large onion, peeled and chopped
1 turnip, peeled and chopped
2 large carrots, peeled and chopped
1 large leek, cleaned and chopped
25 g (1 oz) medium oatmeal
750 ml (1½ pints) stock
Salt and black pepper
2 tablespoons chopped parsley
About 350 ml (½–¾ pint) milk

Melt fat in a pan and sauté the vegetables for 3–4 minutes without browning. Add oatmeal and sauté for a few minutes more, stirring well. Add stock and seasonings and simmer, covered, for about 1 hour till the vegetables are tender. Add parsley, adjust seasonings and add milk. Bring to the boil and serve at once. Serves 6.

TATTIE SOUP

150 g (6 oz) onions, peeled and chopped
1 stick celery, chopped (optional)
40 g (1½ oz) butter or margarine
400 g (1 lb) potatoes, peeled and sliced
1.5 litres (3 pints) white stock
Salt and pepper
1 teaspoon sugar
4–6 tablespoons double (heavy) or sour (dairy sour) cream (optional)
Chopped chives or parsley

Sauté onions and celery if used in butter or margarine for 3–4 minutes without colouring. Add potatoes, stock, salt, pepper and sugar and bring to the boil. Cover and simmer gently for about 1 hour till well broken down and mushy. If a smooth soup is preferred then liquidize or sieve it and return to the pan. Adjust seasonings, stir in cream if required, reheat without boiling, and serve garnished with chives or parsley. Serves 6–8.

Note: For a thinner soup, add milk until the required consistency is obtained.

MUSSEL AND ONION SOUP

If you intend gathering shellfish on the shore or catching crabs in the rocks be sure and seek local advice. Sewage pipes entering the sea in the locality can contaminate shellfish, especially mussels. Also check that you are not interfering with mussels which may have been 'set' by a fisherman as bait for his hooks and lines. All shellfish must be cooked while fresh.

Approx 2 litres (4–5 pints) fresh
  mussels
½ bottle dry white wine
2 large onions, peeled and finely
  chopped
50 g (2 oz) butter
50 g (2 oz) flour
Approx 700 ml (1–1½ pints) milk
Salt and pepper
1 tablespoon lemon juice
2 tablespoons chopped parsley
Approx 200 ml (¼–½ pint) double
  (heavy) cream

Wash and scrub mussels thoroughly, discarding any that are open. Place them in a large pan with the wine and onions. Bring to the boil, cover and simmer very gently for about 10 minutes till all the shells are open. Remove from the liquid and take mussels out of their shells. Melt butter in a pan and stir in the flour. Cook for 1 minute then gradually add the mussel liquor followed by the milk. Bring to the boil, stirring frequently. Season to taste and add lemon juice. Simmer for 5 minutes. Add mussels and continue simmering for 2–3 minutes. Stir in parsley and cream and reheat without boiling. Serves 6–8.

LOBSTER SOUP

1 large boiled lobster shell
Approx 1.5 litres (2-3 pints) fish
  stock or water
Salt and pepper
2 tablespoons chopped onion
1 carrot, peeled and sliced
1 bayleaf
25 g (1 oz) butter
3 tablespoons flour
1 tablespoon lemon juice
125 ml (¼ pint) double (heavy)
  cream
1-2 teaspoons tomato paste
  (optional)
Paprika
Little chopped lobster meat
  (optional)
Lobster coral, sieved (optional)

Remove any pieces of meat from the shell. Wash shell thoroughly then break up. Place the bits in a pan with stock, seasonings, onion, carrot and bayleaf. Bring to the boil, cover and simmer for 45–60 minutes. Strain. Melt butter in a pan and stir in the flour. Cook for 1 minute then slowly add the liquor and bring to the boil, continuing to stir as it thickens. Simmer for 3 minutes then add lemon juice, cream, tomato paste if used, a little paprika and the lobster meat and coral if required. Bring just up to the boil, whisking gently, and serve sprinkled with paprika. Serves 6.

Note: A whole lobster can be used, in which case all the meat is removed and chopped before making the stock and added just before serving. If a smooth soup is required it can be liquidized or sieved.

SALMON SOUP

This is an inexpensive but attractive soup.

Trimmings and head of a salmon
  or sea trout
1 small whiting
Salt and white pepper
1 small bayleaf (optional)
2 carrots, peeled and chopped
2 sticks celery, chopped
1 small onion, peeled and chopped
½ small turnip, peeled and chopped
1.5 litres (3 pints) water
40 g (1½ oz) butter
40 g (1½ oz) flour
1–2 teaspoons lemon juice
Good pinch of ground mace
125 ml (¼ pint) double (heavy)
  cream

Put the bones, fins, skin and head of the salmon or sea trout into a pan with the whiting, salt, pepper, bayleaf if used and vegetables, and amply cover with water. Bring to the boil, skim, and cover. Simmer gently for at least 1 hour. Strain. Melt butter in a pan and stir in the flour. Cook for 1 minute then gradually add the stock. Bring to the boil and simmer for 5 minutes. Add lemon juice, mace, and season to taste. Remove all the flesh from the salmon and a little from the whiting, if liked, and flake finely. Liquidize or sieve soup if preferred. Add cream and reheat without boiling. Serves 4–6.

CULLEN SKINK

1 small or ½ large smoked haddock
1 onion, peeled and chopped
500 ml (1 pint) milk
Salt and pepper
Hot mashed potato
40 g (2 oz) butter

Skin fish and place in a pan with the onion. Cover with water and simmer gently till tender. Remove fish and flake the flesh. Return the bones to the cooking liquor and simmer gently for 1 hour. Strain, return liquor to the pan and add the milk and flaked fish. Bring to the boil and simmer for 5 minutes. Whisk in sufficient mashed potato to give the required consistency. Check seasonings, add butter and reheat before serving. Serves 4–6.

The name of this dish has always fascinated me as 'skink' in Scotland is beef off the leg of a bullock (see Skink Soup, p. 8) and has no connection whatsoever with fish except in this recipe. Furthermore, in spite of much effort I have been unable to find any justification for linking Cullen Skink with the Royal Borough of Cullen in Banffshire. It seems more likely — though I have no real proof — that the dish was named by or after Dr William Cullen. He was born in 1710, and by the 1740s he was a lecturer in chemistry at Glasgow University; being a bon-vivant and gourmet, he became interested in the chemistry of cooking. He invented cream of tartar and was a great advocate of stewing. It seems reasonable to link this fish broth type of dish with the doctor since he also did work on broths and encouraged the eating of them.

PARTAN BREE (CRAB SOUP)

1 medium-sized crab, boiled
60 g (2–2½ oz) rice
500 ml (1 pint) milk
500 ml (1 pint) white stock
Salt and pepper
Paprika
Little anchovy essence or paste
125 ml (¼ pint) double (heavy)
   cream
Chopped parsley

Remove the meat from the large claws, chop roughly and keep aside. Pick out the rest of the meat and chop finely. Boil the rice gently in the milk till tender (about 15 minutes). Add finely chopped crab meat and liquidize or sieve. Place in a pan with the stock, seasoning, and a pinch of paprika and bring very slowly up to the boil. Add a little anchovy essence to taste, and then the claw meat. Simmer for 5–10 minutes, adjust seasonings, stir in cream and reheat without boiling. Serve sprinkled with chopped parsley and paprika. Serves 6.

Note: About 150 g (4–8 oz) frozen crab meat can be used in this recipe when fresh crab is unavailable.

SEAWEED SOUP

Seaweed, like caviare, is an acquired or cultivated taste. The end-product, however, is well worth the effort — the rejuvenating effect of an iron-plus-iodine impregnated food is legendary in places like Ullapool or Buckie: 'A dulsie man's niver oot o' bairns.'

200 g (½ lb) sloke, dulse or
   carrigeen
1.5 litres (3 pints) milk
200 g (½ lb) mashed potatoes
Salt and pepper
25 g (1 oz) butter
2 tablespoons lemon juice

Place the seaweed, milk and potato in a pan and bring to the boil. Simmer for 20–30 minutes then either liquidize or sieve or beat hard till smooth. Return to the pan, season to taste, add butter and lemon juice and bring back to the boil. Simmer for a few minutes before serving. Serves 6–8.

Note: Use dried seaweed if the fresh is unavailable.

FISH

Fish is fresh and plentiful all over Scotland. Most of it is caught by inshore boats which go to sea for only one or two days at a time, and their catch is usually of a higher quality than the landings made by long-distance trawlers which stay at sea from ten to fourteen days and bring their haul back to the ports on ice. However, modern freezing plants at the point of landing now make it possible for fresh Scottish fish to be enjoyed over a wide area.

Fresh-caught herrings, split, cleaned, steeped in brine for a short while and smoke-cured over wood chips, give us the Scottish kipper, possibly one of the attractive forms of fish eaten anywhere. Before the serious decline in the herring shoals, salt herrings too were very popular, at one time exported in vast quantities to the Baltic ports. Today, unfortunately, they are difficult to find, but if you are lucky enough to trace a supply, try a 'tattie-and-herring supper', the traditional autumn feast in the herring ports: soak the fish in fresh water for twenty-four hours, then boil in unsalted water and serve with boiled potatoes in their jackets (see p. 69).

The main catch in Scottish waters nowadays is cod, followed by haddock, the favourite of the inshore boat. These fish, and whiting, used to be preserved by sun-drying, but now, as with kippers, wood-smoking is the common method. The very lightly smoked 'Finnan' haddock takes its name from the village of Findon in Kincardineshire, but haddocks are cured all along the coasts, varying greatly in colour and density of smoking.

Scottish salmon is reputed to be the best in the world, whether eaten fresh or smoked. They are caught by rod and line in the rivers, and in large quantities by nets at the estuaries.

The reduction in the herring catch has meant that other fish which traditionally were not highly regarded — mainly mackerel and sprats — have increased in importance. At one time, Scottish fishermen were very reluctant to land mackerel at all, maintaining it would spoil unless eaten immediately it was got ashore. New freezing methods have of course helped to break down this old prejudice. Over the years, there has also been a reluctance among the Scottish public as a whole to eat shellfish; but there are now signs of a growing appreciation of the plentiful supplies around the coast. If you want to gather any yourself, you should first check with local residents that the shellfish are free from pollution and are not private property. Many varieties of seaweed can also be gathered almost anywhere along the Scottish coast (use in Seaweed Soup, p. 13), but again, do ask for local advice.

KIPPERS

Kippers can be bought fresh, quick-frozen, as canned fillets, or in boil-in-the-bag packs. They can be boiled, grilled, fried, baked, jugged or boiled-in-the-bag. If the head is still on when you buy the kipper, remove it and trim the tail if preferred.

To boil: Place in a pan of gently simmering water, bring back to the boil, and simmer for 5 minutes.

To grill: Place on the rack under a moderately heated grill, skin side up, for about 3–5 minutes. Turn and grill the fleshy side for 5–6 minutes till the bone leaves the flesh. Do not overcook or the fish will become dry and hard.

To fry: Fry gently in very little fat in a shallow pan for about 4 minutes on each side. Kippers can be dipped in boiling water before frying to remove some of the saltiness, but you may feel that this detracts from the flavour.

To bake: Place kippers in pairs flesh sides together, in foil or in a heatproof dish. Package foil loosely or cover the dish, and cook at 200°C (400°F, Gas 6) for 15–20 minutes.

To jug: Place kippers in a jug or bowl and pour boiling water over them till well covered. Cover tightly and leave to stand for 10–15 minutes. Drain and serve.

To boil-in-the-bag: Follow the instructions on the pack. If these are not given, simmer in the bag for about 7 minutes.

Note: If the after-cooking smell of kippers troubles you, add 1 teaspoon of dry mustard to the washing-up water, which should be really hot.

KIPPER TOASTS

2 kippers
Good pinch of cayenne pepper
12 g (½ oz) butter
2–3 slices buttered toast
Mustard
Parsley sprigs
1 tomato, sliced

Cook the kippers by the method preferred then strip flesh from the skin and bones and flake into a bowl. Mash thoroughly, then beat in cayenne and butter. Spread toast lightly with mustard then pile kipper mixture on top. Place under a hot grill for a few minutes to heat through then serve quickly with parsley and tomato for garnish. Serves 2–3.

KIPPER PÂTÉ

6 kipper fillets, approx 200 g (8 oz)
50 g (2 oz) butter
1 small onion, peeled and very finely chopped
¼ teaspoon grated lemon rind
2 teaspoons lemon juice
Freshly ground black pepper
2–3 tablespoons double (heavy) cream
Watercress

Cook kipper fillets in gently boiling water for about 5 minutes till tender, then drain, remove skin and any bones and flake into a bowl. Beat in the butter, onion, lemon rind and juice and freshly ground pepper to taste. Either sieve, blend in a liquidizer or beat hard till smooth. Add more pepper to taste if necessary, beat in cream and chill thoroughly before serving with hot toast or oatcakes and garnished with watercress.

KILTED KIPPERS

This was new to me when it was served as a savoury at a dinner in the Caledonian Club in London some years ago. I have given it the name — 'Kilted Kippers'. The streaky bacon wrapped round the kipper does look like a kilt!

4–8 kipper fillets
Black pepper
Lemon juice
8–16 rashers streaky bacon, derinded

Cut each fillet into 2 or 3 pieces and sprinkle lightly with pepper and lemon juice. Wrap pieces of streaky bacon round the kippers and impale on skewers. Place under a low to medium grill and cook, turning once, till the bacon is browned and the kipper is cooked through. Serve with lemon wedges and brown bread and butter. Serves 4–8.

FRIED HERRINGS IN OATMEAL

4 herrings, cleaned
Salt and pepper
6–8 tablespoons medium oatmeal
Fat or oil for frying

Remove heads, fins and tails of fish and the bone. To remove the backbone from a herring, slit along the stomach then place flesh side down and press thumbs firmly along the skin over the backbone to loosen it. Turn over and ease the bone out. Wipe and dry fish. Season with salt and pepper and dip in the oatmeal, pressing it well in. Fry in fat or shallow oil for about 5–6 minutes each side. Drain on absorbent paper and serve very hot with boiled potatoes and lemon wedges.

Note: The roes can be coated and fried in the same way. Some cooks dip the herring into seasoned milk or beaten egg before the oatmeal to help it stick but this is not really necessary.

HERRING ROES ON OATCAKES

300 g (12 oz) soft herring roes
25 g (1 oz) butter
Salt and pepper
1 teaspoon lemon juice
2 teaspoons freshly chopped
   parsley (optional)
2–3 oatcakes or slices of toast
Little butter or margarine

Wash roes carefully then drain and dry as well as possible. Melt butter in a pan and add the roes. Cook gently for about 5–10 minutes till lightly browned. Stir carefully to prevent breaking up. Season with salt and pepper and add lemon juice and parsley. Spread oatcakes or toast with butter or margarine and pile roes on top. Dot with butter and put under a hot grill for a few minutes till sizzling. Serve with lemon wedges. Serves 2–3.

POTTED HERRINGS

4–8 herrings
Salt and freshly ground black
  pepper
250 ml ($\frac{1}{2}$ pint) water
250 ml ($\frac{1}{2}$ pint) vinegar
2 bayleaves
4 cloves
1 blade of mace
Few black peppercorns
1 large onion, peeled and thinly
  sliced

Prepare and bone herrings as for Fried Herrings in
Oatmeal (see p. 16). Sprinkle insides with salt and
pepper and roll up tightly from tail to head with skin
outside. Pack into a heatproof dish. Cover fish with
equal quantities of water and vinegar (half malt and
half tarragon vinegar gives an excellent flavour). Add
bayleaves, cloves, mace, peppercorns and onion and
cover with buttered foil or greaseproof paper. Cook
at 150°C (300°F, Gas 2) for about 1$\frac{1}{2}$ hours till tender.
Cool in the liquor and serve cold with salad.

BAKED STUFFED HERRINGS

4 herrings, cleaned
25 g (1 oz) butter
1 onion, peeled and chopped
75 g (3 oz) mushrooms, chopped
1 tablespoon chopped parsley
$\frac{1}{4}$ teaspoon grated lemon rind
40 g (1$\frac{1}{2}$ oz) fresh breadcrumbs
Salt and pepper
1 egg, beaten

Remove heads and bone herrings as for Fried Herrings
in Oatmeal (see p. 16). Reserve any roes and chop.
Melt butter and fry onion till soft then add mushrooms
and continue for 2–3 minutes. Add roes and cook for
a further 2 minutes. Remove from heat and stir in
parsley, lemon rind, breadcrumbs and seasonings, and
bind together with the egg. Stuff the fish, fold back
into shape and put each one in an individual piece of
foil and package loosely. Alternatively put all the fish
into a lightly greased, covered, heatproof dish. Bake
the fish at 180°C (350°F, Gas 4) for 25–30 minutes till
cooked through and tender.

Note: Mackerel can be cooked in the same way.

STUFFED COD CUTLETS

4 cod cutlets
Salt and pepper
1 onion, peeled and chopped
40 g (1$\frac{1}{2}$ oz) butter
50 g (2 oz) mushrooms, chopped
1 tablespoon parsley
1–2 tomatoes, peeled and chopped
50 g (2 oz) fresh breadcrumbs
1 tablespoon capers, chopped
4 fillets anchovies, drained and
  chopped (optional)

Wipe cutlets and carefully remove the backbone.
Season fish well. Fry onion in butter for about 2
minutes then add mushrooms and continue for a
further 2 minutes. Stir in seasonings, parsley, tomatoes,
breadcrumbs, capers, and anchovies if used. Fill the
holes left after removing bones and fold flaps of fish
round to enclose filling. Place any remaining filling on
top of cutlets. Secure with wooden cocktail sticks or
string. Place in a lightly greased dish and cook at 200°C
(400°F, Gas 6) for 20–30 minutes, depending on the
thickness of the fish, till tender.

COD AND CAPER SOUFFLÉ

400 g (1 lb) cod fillet
Salt and pepper
1½ teaspoons lemon juice
100 g (4 oz) butter or margarine
1 onion, peeled and chopped
75 g (3 oz) flour
375 ml (¾ pint) milk
Pinch of ground mace
2–3 tablespoons capers, drained
   and chopped
3 eggs, separated
2 tablespoons grated Parmesan
   cheese

Poach the fish in lightly seasoned water with the lemon juice till tender — 10–15 minutes. Drain well, remove skin and bones from fish and flake. Melt butter in a pan and sauté onion till soft. Stir in flour and cook for 1 minute. Gradually add the milk and bring to the boil, stirring continuously. Season with salt, pepper and mace and stir in fish and capers. Beat in the egg yolks one at a time. Beat egg whites till very stiff and fold into the mixture. Pour into a well greased 2 litre (4 pint) soufflé dish, filling it two-thirds full. Sprinkle with Parmesan cheese and cook at 180°C (350°F, Gas 4) for about 1 hour till golden brown and firm to the touch. Serve immediately or soufflé will sink and become tough.

Note: For a change, a mixture of white fish and shellfish or smoked fish can also be used in this recipe.

COD'S ROE WITH BACON

400 g (1 lb) fresh cod's roe
Salted water
1–2 tablespoons vinegar
200 g (½ lb) bacon rashers,
   derinded
Seasoned flour

Cod's roe is often bought ready boiled; if not, wash carefully, then, if the skin is broken, tie the roe in muslin. Simmer gently in salted water with the vinegar for 25–30 minutes. Drain and cool. Remove muslin carefully and cut roe into slices when cold. Fry the bacon quickly, adding a little fat or oil to the pan if necessary. Remove and keep warm. Dip roe in seasoned flour and fry in the bacon fat till golden brown on each side. Drain well and serve on a dish surrounded by bacon.

Note: The roe can be dipped in egg and crumbed, or dipped in flour and fritter batter, and fried in deep or shallow fat. Serve with lemon and a piquant sauce. Cod's roe is also available in cans when it is simply removed, sliced, and cooked. Freshly boiled cod's roe will freeze well and can be cut into slices before freezing.

BAKED COD WITH MUSTARD SAUCE

4 cod cutlets or pieces of fillet,
    approx 600 g (1½ lb)
Salt and pepper
Good squeeze of lemon juice
250 ml (½ pint) milk
40 g (1½ oz) butter
40 g (1½ oz) flour
1–1½ tablespoons dry mustard or
    French or German mustard
1–1½ tablespoons vinegar
2 teaspoons sugar
Lemon wedges for garnish

Place fish in a lightly buttered heatproof dish and season well with salt and pepper. Add lemon juice and milk and cover. Cook at 180°C (350°F, Gas 4) for 30–40 minutes till tender. Drain off liquor and make up to 375 ml (¾ pint) with more milk if necessary. Keep fish warm. Melt butter in a pan, stir in flour and cook for 1 minute. Gradually add fish liquor and bring to the boil. Add mustard, vinegar, sugar and seasonings to taste. Simmer for 3 minutes. Serve fish with the sauce, garnished with lemon wedges.

Note: More mustard and vinegar can be added to give a really strong piquant taste. The fish can also be grilled and served with the same sauce.

TIED TAILIES (ARBROATH SMOKIES)

Arbroath Smokies are, by tradition, smoked haddock, but you sometimes find whitings used: you can always tell the difference by looking for the 'St Peter's thumb-mark' behind the gills of haddock.

These are quite unlike any other smoked fish. They are very small haddock, cleaned but not split open, and salted. They are tied in pairs by the tails for smoking (hence the name 'Tied Tailies') and smoked usually over oak or silver birch chips. The finished fish has a copper coloured outside and the flesh has a creamy texture and savoury flavour. They are best eaten without cooking, the tough skin being peeled off before serving with lemon wedges and horseradish sauce.

Note: Smoked mackerel, a new phenomenon in Scottish fish shops, is almost as tasty as an Arbroath Smokie or smoked trout or salmon. Serve in the same way as smokies.

SOURED HADDOCK

Approx 550 g (1¼–1½ lb) haddock
    fillets, fresh or smoked
Salt and pepper
40 g (1½ oz) butter
1 onion, peeled and finely
    chopped
100 g (4 oz) button mushrooms,
    sliced
250 ml (½ pint) soured cream
    (see note below)
1½ tablespoons lemon juice
1 tablespoon wine or cider
    vinegar
¾ teaspoon paprika
1–2 teaspoons dried marjoram
1 lemon or 2 tomatoes for garnish

Poach haddock in a little lightly seasoned water for about 15 minutes until tender. Drain well and keep warm. Melt butter in a pan and fry onion slowly till just beginning to colour. Add mushrooms and continue for 2 minutes, stirring frequently. Stir in soured cream, lemon juice, vinegar, salt and pepper, paprika and marjoram. Allow sauce to simmer very gently for about 10 minutes. Serve fish on a dish masked with the sauce and garnished with wedges of lemon or tomato.

Note: To sour cream add 1–2 teaspoons of lemon juice to 125 ml (¼ pint) of single (light) cream.

HAM AND HADDIE

4–8 small smoked haddock fillets
40 g (1½ oz) butter
8 smoked back rashers of bacon,
    derinded
Black pepper
Little whipped cream (optional)

Poach the fish gently in a little water for 3–4 minutes then drain and keep hot. Melt butter in a pan and fry bacon quickly till crisp. Dip fish into the bacon fat in the pan and fry for a minute or two, adding a little black pepper. Serve on hot dishes topped with the fried bacon and, if liked, a spoonful of whipped cream.

Note: The pale Morav . . . ked haddocks are the best for this recipe, though an   ed haddock can be used.

FINDON OR FINNAN TOASTS

200 g (½ lb) Finnan-Haddie
    (smoked haddock)
A little milk and water
25 g (1 oz) butter
2–4 gherkins, finely chopped
3–4 tablespoons double (heavy)
    cream
Salt and pepper
Pinch of cayenne pepper
2–3 slices fried bread or toast
Chopped parsley

Place haddock in a pan with a little milk and enough water to just cover fish. Simmer gently for about 10 minutes then drain. Remove skin and bones and flake fish. Melt butter in a pan and add the haddock, gherkins, cream and seasonings to taste. Heat thoroughly, stirring gently. Pile quickly onto the hot fried bread or toast. Garnish with parsley and serve immediately for a snack or part of a meal. Serves 2–3.

FRIED HADDOCK

4 pieces filleted fresh haddock,
    approx 600 g (1½ lb)
Salt and pepper
1 egg, beaten
Golden breadcrumbs or raspings
Fat or oil for frying

Wipe the fish and season lightly with salt and pepper. Dip each piece of fish into beaten egg then coat thoroughly in breadcrumbs. Fry in hot shallow fat in a frying pan for about 5 minutes each side or fry in hot deep fat for 4–5 minutes till golden brown and cooked through. Drain well on absorbent paper and serve hot with lemon wedges, parsley and bread and butter for high tea.

SMOKED HADDOCK WITH CHEESE

600 g (1½ lb) smoked haddock
500 ml (1 pint) milk
50 g (2 oz) butter
1 onion, peeled and chopped
2 tablespoons flour
Salt and pepper
40 g (2 oz) grated Cheddar
    cheese
600 g (1½ lb) creamed potatoes
6 tomatoes, skinned and sliced
1–2 tablespoons Parmesan cheese

Boil the fish in milk till tender then strain off liquor. Skin, bone and flake fish. Melt butter in a pan and sauté onion gently till soft but not coloured. Stir in flour and cook for 1 minute. Gradually add milk and bring to the boil, stirring frequently. Season to taste and simmer for 3 minutes. Stir in Cheddar cheese. Lightly butter a heatproof dish. Pipe or spread a border of potato around the dish and fill with layers of flaked fish, tomatoes and sauce. Finish with a layer of sauce, sprinkle with Parmesan cheese and cook at 200°C (400°F, Gas 6) for about 30 minutes till heated through and browned on top. Flash under a hot grill to brown up if necessary.

STUFFED HADDOCK

Approx 1 kg (2–2½ lb) fresh
    filleted haddock
60 g (2½ oz) butter
1 small onion, peeled and
    chopped
2 rashers bacon, chopped
1 clove garlic, crushed (optional)
1 hardboiled egg, chopped
1 tablespoon chopped parsley or
    1 teaspoon chopped dill
Salt and pepper
1 tablespoon lemon juice
50 g (2 oz) fresh breadcrumbs
40 g (1½ oz) flour
½ teaspoon dry mustard
250 ml (½ pint) milk
50 g (2 oz) grated Cheddar cheese

Melt 25 g (1 oz) of butter and fry onion, bacon, and garlic if used till soft. Add egg, parsley or dill, salt, pepper, lemon juice and breadcrumbs, and mix well. Put the stuffing into the middle of the fish, folding over flaps to enclose it, and secure with string. Place fish on well greased foil and package loosely, or place in a well buttered heatproof dish and cover. Bake at 190°C (375°F, Gas 5) for about 1 hour till tender. Melt the remaining butter in a pan, stir in the flour and mustard and cook for 1 minute. Make the liquid from the fish up to 375 ml (¾ pint) with milk, add to the roux and bring to the boil. Season to taste and simmer for 3 minutes. Stir in the cheese till it melts, and either pour the sauce over the fish or serve separately.

HALIBUT

4 halibut steaks
125 ml ($\frac{1}{4}$ pint) dry white wine
Salt and pepper
Bouquet garni (see p. 3)
1 small onion, peeled and finely
   chopped
40 g ($1\frac{1}{2}$ oz) butter
1 tablespoon flour
4 tablespoons tomato paste
125 ml ($\frac{1}{4}$ pint) water
2–3 tomatoes, skinned and
   chopped (optional)
1 lemon and parsley sprigs for garnish

Wipe fish and place in a shallow pan with the wine, seasonings and bouquet garni. Poach gently for about 20 minutes till tender. Drain fish and keep warm. Fry onion in the butter till lightly brown then stir in flour and tomato paste. Cook for 1 minute then gradually add strained fish cooking liquor, and water. Add tomatoes if used, bring to the boil and simmer gently for 5–10 minutes. Adjust seasonings and pour over the fish. Garnish with lemon twists and parsley.

Note: Cod or haddock fillet can be cooked in the same way.

HALIBUT WITH SHRIMP SAUCE

4 halibut steaks, approx 150 g
   (6 oz) each
125 ml ($\frac{1}{4}$ pint) milk
Salt and pepper
50 g (2 oz) butter
25 g (1 oz) flour
100 g (4 oz) peeled shrimps or
   prawns
1–2 teaspoons lemon juice
Parsley sprigs
Few whole shrimps or prawns
   (optional)

Lightly butter a heatproof dish and place the halibut in it. Pour the milk over the fish, season and dot with half the butter. Cook uncovered at 180°C (350°F, Gas 4) for 20–25 minutes till cooked through. Drain off liquor and make up to 250 ml ($\frac{1}{2}$ pint) with more milk. Keep fish warm. Melt remaining butter in a pan, stir in the flour and cook for 1 minute. Gradually add the liquor and bring to the boil, stirring frequently. Add shrimps and lemon juice, check seasonings and simmer for 3 minutes. Pour over halibut and garnish with parsley and a few whole shrimps or prawns if required.

BOILED SKATE

800 g (2 lb) skate (slices from
   larger wings)
1 litre (2 pints) fish stock or
   water
Salt and pepper
75 g (3 oz) butter
2 tablespoons vinegar (preferably
   wine or cider)
1–2 tablespoons capers
1 tablespoon chopped parsley
Lemon wedges

Wash and trim the fish and place in a pan with stock or water to cover. Season lightly. Bring to the boil and simmer very gently for 15 minutes. Drain and keep warm. Melt butter in a frying pan and heat till it turns a deep golden brown. Pour over the fish. Add vinegar to the same pan and swirl round for 1–2 minutes. Pour over fish. Sprinkle with capers and parsley, add lemon wedges and serve with boiled potatoes.

Note: Small pieces of wing are excellent shallow fried or coated in batter and deep fried. Pieces from large wings should be boiled for 10 minutes before frying.

Top: Fried Steaks (p. 46), fried potatoes and Skirlie (p. 78).

Bottom: **Savoury** Mince (p. 40) with boiled potatoes and Pickled Beetroot (p. 70).

FRIED PLAICE

4 small whole plaice or 8 small
  fillets
Seasoned flour
1 egg, beaten
Golden breadcrumbs or raspings
Oil or fat for frying

Wipe fish, remove skin if preferred, then coat in seasoned flour. Dip in beaten egg, then coat in breadcrumbs, pressing well in to give an even covering. If using deep fat, heat and fry whole fish for about 5 minutes and fillets for 2–3 minutes. In shallow fat whole fish are fried for 5 minutes each side and fillets for 3–4 minutes each side. Drain on absorbent paper and serve with lemon and a tartare (see p. 32) or other piquant sauce. The fish can also be placed in a greased baking tin, topped with a few knobs of butter, and cooked at 200°C (400°F, Gas 6) for 20–30 minutes.

Note: Lemon sole, flounders and dabs can be cooked in the same way. Plaice and fillets can also be coated in batter and fried in deep fat.

PLAICE ROLLS

50 g (2 oz) Cheddar cheese,
  grated
2 hardboiled eggs, chopped
1 tablespoon chopped parsley
50 g (2 oz) fresh breadcrumbs
50 g (2 oz) peeled prawns
  (optional)
Salt and pepper
50 g (2 oz) melted butter
2 large plaice, filleted and skinned
Approx 125 ml ($\frac{1}{4}$ pint) milk
25 g (1 oz) butter
25 g (1 oz) flour
2 tablespoons white wine
  (optional)

Combine cheese, eggs, parsley, 40 g ($1\frac{1}{2}$ oz) breadcrumbs, prawns if used and seasonings, and bind with melted butter. Spread the mixture over the skin side of the fillets and roll up tightly. Place in a lightly buttered ovenproof dish, sprinkle with remaining crumbs and cook at 180°C (350°F, Gas 4) for about 25 minutes till fish is tender and crumbs browned on top. Strain off liquor and make up to 250 ml ($\frac{1}{2}$ pint) with milk. Melt butter in a pan, add flour and cook for 1 minute. Gradually add liquor and bring to the boil. Add wine if required, season to taste and simmer for 3 minutes. Serve fish with the sauce separately.

Boiled Hen (p. 51) with Chappet Tatties (p. 73), Oatmeal and
Onion Stuffing (p. 56), Bread Sauce (p. 57) and Oatcakes (p. 79).

FRIED WHITING WITH ORANGE SAUCE

4 fresh whiting, filleted or whole
3 Seville oranges or 2 sweet
  oranges and 1 lemon
3 egg yolks
4 tablespoons double (heavy)
  cream
Bare 125 ml ($\frac{1}{4}$ pint) dry white
  wine
Salt and pepper
Cayenne pepper
100 g (4 oz) butter
Little seasoned flour
Chopped parsley

Sprinkle fish with the juice of $\frac{1}{2}$ an orange (or $\frac{1}{2}$ the lemon). Leave in a cool place. Beat together egg yolks, cream, wine and juice of $1\frac{1}{2}$ Seville oranges (or 1 orange and $\frac{1}{2}$ the lemon). Stand bowl over a pan of gently simmering water and stir the mixture till it has the consistency of thick pouring cream. Season with salt, pepper and cayenne, then gradually beat in 50 g (2 oz) butter in small pieces. Keep warm without continuing to cook. Dip whiting in seasoned flour and fry in remaining melted butter for 5–8 minutes each side for a whole fish, and rather less for a fillet. Arrange on a serving dish with the remaining orange cut into slices and sprinkled with parsley. Serve sauce separately.

SIMPLE SOLE

4 small sole, skinned and cleaned
Seasoned flour
75 g (3 oz) butter
1–2 tablespoons chopped parsley
Juice of 1 lemon
1 lemon, sliced, for garnish

Wipe the fish and coat thoroughly in seasoned flour. Heat 50 g (2 oz) butter in a frying pan and put in the fish. Fry for about 5 minutes till golden brown then turn them over carefully and continue for 5 minutes till tender and cooked through. Remove to a serving dish and keep warm. Wipe out pan then melt remaining butter in it and heat until lightly browned. Add parsley and lemon juice and pour immediately over the fish. Garnish with lemon.

Note: All types of sole as well as plaice can be cooked in this way.

SALMON

There are several methods of cooking salmon and sea trout (sometimes called salmon trout by the fishmonger). If it is not already prepared, first scale it holding it by the tail and scraping towards the head with a knife. Gut it, then scrape and wash away all the blood. Salmon may be poached, baked or grilled, whole, in large pieces or in steaks.

Poached Salmon

For a whole salmon, large piece of salmon or a sea trout, half-fill a fish kettle with water and add about 200 ml ($\frac{1}{4}$–$\frac{1}{2}$ pint) white wine, salt, 1 sliced onion, 1 blade of mace and a bouquet garni (see p. 3). Bring just up to simmering point and lower in the fish. Return to the boil and simmer (the water should only just shimmer) allowing 10 minutes per 400 g (1 lb) plus 10 minutes. Remove carefully from the water and skin. Serve hot with Hollandaise sauce (see p. 33), lemon wedges, cucumber and boiled potatoes. When serving cold, either remove from water and leave till cold before skinning, or simmer for just 10 minutes per 400 g (1 lb) and leave to cool in the water. Serve either coated in aspic or just decorated and served with mayonnaise. To cook a 1 kg (2–2$\frac{1}{2}$ lb) piece of salmon and serve cold, simmer in a smaller pan for 10–15 minutes and leave to cool in the water. Poach salmon steaks in a covered frying pan as above for 5–10 minutes.

Baked Salmon

This method can be used for a piece of salmon of any size that will fit into the oven. Clean and prepare fish and place 1–2 bayleaves (optional), salt and pepper, squeeze of lemon juice and a knob of butter inside it. Rub a large piece of foil with butter and sprinkle with salt and pepper. Place fish on foil. curling it round in the case of a large or whole fish to give an attractive shape when cooked and to enable the largest possible fish to fit in the oven. Package foil loosely, stand on a baking sheet and cook at 150°C (300°F, Gas 2) for about 1 hour, for a fish around 1.5 kg (2–4 lb), depending on thickness. Cool in foil, skin and serve as for poached salmon. If serving hot allow an extra 5–10 minutes' cooking and cool in foil for 10 minutes before skinning and serving.

Note: If the whole fish is too large to fit into a fish kettle or oven, it can be cut into 2–3 pieces and wrapped individually in foil before cooking, then served reassembled with the joins hidden by decorations.

SMOKED SALMON

This is a great favourite with many but a rather expensive delicacy. The whole smoked sides of salmon are displayed and the amount required cut off as needed by the customer. It can also be bought pre-packed for the deep freezer from fish shops and delicatessens. Sometimes the tail slices are inclined to be salt, so avoid them if you don't like this. You can also buy a whole side of smoked salmon if you are having a party. The fishmonger should bone it for you and advise you on storing.

The salmon must be cut in wafer-thin slices along the length of the fish. Allow about 50 g (2 oz) per person and serve it laid out on a plate garnished with parsley sprigs and lemon wedges with very thinly sliced brown bread and butter. Also offer freshly ground black or red pepper.

SALMON MOUSSE

25 g (1 oz) butter
25 g (1 oz) flour
250 ml (bare ½ pint) milk
¼ teaspoon dry mustard
Good pinch of cayenne
Salt and pepper
1½ tablespoons wine vinegar
3 eggs, separated
300 g (12 oz) cooked salmon, flaked
4 tablespoons double (heavy) cream
1½ tablespoons powdered gelatine
5 tablespoons water

Melt butter in a pan, stir in flour and cook for 1 minute. Gradually add milk and bring to the boil. Add mustard, cayenne, salt and pepper to taste, and vinegar and simmer for 3 minutes. Beat in egg yolks and simmer for 2 minutes. Stir in flaked salmon and cream. Dissolve gelatine in a small basin with the water and stir into the salmon mixture. Leave till on the point of setting then fold in stiffly beaten egg whites. Pour into a bowl or lightly greased mould and leave to set. Garnish dish or turned out mould with asparagus spears, or cucumber and olives.

Note: A combination of fish can be used in this recipe, such as salmon and white fish; smoked or canned salmon and white fish; or it can be made completely with canned salmon.

SMOKED TROUT

Allow one small — 200 g (8 oz) — trout per person. The head and tail are left in place and the skin is usually removed. However, this must be done at the last possible moment to prevent the flesh from drying out. Serve with lemon wedges, horseradish cream or sauce, and brown bread and butter. Smoked trout can be bought fresh or frozen. If you are lucky enough to have someone in the family who catches trout, you can smoke your own, freshly caught, on a home kit available with maker's instructions from many large stores). This uses sawdust and will also smoke many other foods, such as sausages and chicken breasts, with delicious results.

TROUT WITH ALMONDS

4 rainbow trout, each 200 g (8 oz)
Salt and pepper
75 g (3 oz) butter
50 g (2 oz) blanched or flaked almonds
2 tablespoons lemon juice
4–6 tablespoons cream (optional)
Chopped parsley

Wipe trout (leaving heads on) and season lightly with salt and pepper. Either brush with a little melted butter and place in a grill pan, or place in a frying pan with a little melted butter. Grill or fry for 5–10 minutes, turning once, till cooked through. Meanwhile melt 50 g (2 oz) butter in a pan and add the almonds. Fry gently till pale brown, shaking pan frequently. Remove from heat and add lemon juice. Cool slightly and add cream if used and reheat without boiling. Season to taste. Serve trout with sauce spooned over and sprinkled with parsley.

FISH CAKES

400 g (1 lb) smoked haddock
125 ml (¼ pint) milk
2 tablespoons parsley
1–2 hardboiled eggs, chopped
Salt and pepper
400 g (1 lb) mashed potatoes
Golden breadcrumbs or raspings
Fat or oil for frying

Place fish in a pan with the milk and enough water to just cover. Simmer gently for about 10 minutes then drain. Remove skin and bones and flake fish into a bowl. Mix in parsley, chopped egg, seasonings and potato, moistening with a little of the cooking liquor if necessary. Divide into 8–12 pieces and form into flat round cakes. Dip thoroughly in breadcrumbs then fry in shallow fat for about 5–7 minutes each side till golden brown, or place in a well greased baking tin and cook at 200°C (400°F, Gas 6) for about 30 minutes, turning once. Serves 4–6.

FISHERMAN'S PIE

200 g (½ lb) white fish (cod, haddock)
Salt and pepper
250 ml (½ pint) milk
25 g (1 oz) butter
1 small onion, peeled and chopped
3 tablespoons flour
Good pinch of cayenne
2 tablespoons chopped parsley or 2 teaspoons dill
1 hardboiled egg, chopped
150 g (4–6 oz) puff pastry (see p. 97)
Beaten egg to glaze

Poach fish in 125 ml (¼ pint) seasoned milk till tender, then drain and make liquor up to 250 ml (½ pint) with more milk. Melt butter and fry onion for 3–4 minutes without colouring. Stir in flour, cook for 1 minute then gradually add the measured cooking liquor. Bring to the boil, season well with salt, pepper and cayenne and simmer for 3 minutes. Skin and flake fish and add parsley or dill, and egg. Mix in half the sauce and leave to cool. Roll out pastry thinly to a large square, trim, and place on a baking sheet. Place filling in the middle in a square shape. Brush edges of pastry with beaten egg and draw up to the middle to make an envelope shape. Press edges well together then flake with a sharp knife and crimp. Brush with egg and cook at 200°C (400°F, Gas 6) for about 30 minutes till golden brown. Serve with remaining sauce, reheated and thinned with a little more milk if necessary.

Note: This mixture can be put into a dish, topped with mashed potato and cooked as above. Additions such as shelled prawns or shrimps, chopped tomatoes or cheese can be added and smoked haddock can replace the white fish.

SKIPPER'S PIE

400 g (1 lb) fresh haddock or cod fillet, skinned
Salt and pepper
250 (½ pint) milk
1 small onion, peeled and chopped
Bouquet garni (see p. 3)
100 g (4 oz) shelled prawns or shrimps
Small jar mussels, drained (or use cooked fresh ones)
25 g (1 oz) butter
25 g (1 oz) flour
2 teaspoons anchovy essence or 8 anchovy fillets, chopped
600 g (1½ lb) creamed potatoes
Little beaten egg (optional)

Poach the fish in seasoned milk with the onion and bouquet garni for about 10 minutes. Remove bouquet garni and strain off liquor. Make up to 250 ml (½ pint) with water or more milk. Flake fish roughly and mix with prawns or shrimps and mussels. Melt butter, stir in flour and cook for 1 minute. Gradually add liquor and bring to the boil. Simmer for 3 minutes then add anchovy essence or fillets, season to taste and add the mixed fish. Pour into a heatproof dish and pipe over it a thick border of potato (or cover entirely with potato). Brush the potato with egg, if liked, and cook at 200°C (400°F, Gas 6) for about 20 minutes till browned.

MACKEREL WITH GOOSEBERRY SAUCE

1 mackerel per serving
Salt and pepper
Lemon juice
Oil
Approx half a dozen goose-
   berries per serving
Sugar
Lemon rind

After gutting, wash the fish and remove heads. Season the insides and sprinkle with lemon juice. Brush the outsides with oil, and cook in one of the following ways: grill for 7–8 minutes on each side till cooked through; or fry gently for 6–8 minutes each side; or bake in the oven at 180°C (350°F, Gas 4) for about 30 minutes. Top, tail, and wash gooseberries and simmer in water till tender. Liquidize or sieve and return to the pan with sugar to taste and lemon rind. Serve the fish with the sauce, or hand the sauce separately.

Note: Mackerel can also be scored and soaked in a marinade for an hour before grilling.

LOBSTER

Most lobsters are sold ready-boiled, but if you have to cook a live one, the boiling process is quite simple. Fill a large pan with cold, well salted water. Weigh the lobster, then put it in the pan and cover (weight the lid to stop the lobster jumping out!). Bring slowly up to simmering point and allow 15 minutes for the first 400 g (1 lb) and 10 minutes after that for each 400 g (1 lb). Do not overcook or the flesh will become hard and thready. Remove the lobster, and allow to cool. Fresh lobster is black, while cooked lobster is red.

To serve cold: Remove the claws, then split the lobster lengthwise with a strong pointed knife. Remove the intestine, which is like a small vein running through the centre of the tail, the stomach, which lies near the head, and the spongy-looking gills. Stand the lobster on a bed of lettuce with the claws rearranged around it. Serve with mayonnaise and salads.

OBAN LOBSTER

2 cooked lobsters, approx 300 g
   ($\frac{3}{4}$ lb) each
60 g (2$\frac{1}{2}$ oz) butter
1 tablespoon finely chopped
   shallot or onion
2 teaspoons chopped parsley
Good pinch of chopped tarragon
4 tablespoons white wine
25 g (1 oz) flour
200 ml ($\frac{1}{4}$ pint+4 tablespoons)
   milk
Salt and pepper
125 ml ($\frac{1}{4}$ pint) double (heavy)
   cream
$\frac{1}{4}$–$\frac{1}{2}$ teaspoon dry mustard
Good pinch of paprika
3 tablespoons grated Parmesan
   cheese

Split the lobsters in half lengthwise and remove the intestine, the stomach and the gills (see previous recipe). Remove the lobster meat from the shell, chopping claw and head meat and thickly slicing the tail meat. Melt 40 g (1$\frac{1}{2}$ oz) butter in a pan and add shallot or onion, parsley and tarragon. Sauté for a few minutes, then add the wine and simmer for 5 minutes. Make a white sauce using the remaining butter, flour and milk. Stir in the wine mixture, and season to taste, adding cream, mustard, paprika and 1–2 tablespoons Parmesan cheese. Bring to the boil, add the lobster meat and simmer gently for 3 minutes. Spoon the mixture back into the shells, sprinkle with the remaining cheese and brown lightly under the grill.

Note: This dish can be prepared in advance and reheated at 180°C (350°F, Gas 4) for about 20–30 minutes and then browned under the grill before serving. A mixture of Cheddar and Parmesan cheese can be used if preferred.

PARTAN FLAN (CRAB FLAN)

150 g (6 oz) plain flour
Pinch of salt
40 g (1$\frac{1}{2}$ oz) margarine
40 g (1$\frac{1}{2}$ oz) lard (shortening)
Water to mix
200 g (8 oz) crab meat
2 tablespoons finely grated onion
2 eggs
Salt and pepper
Good pinch of cayenne pepper
125 ml ($\frac{1}{4}$ pint) milk
125 ml ($\frac{1}{4}$ pint) double (heavy)
   cream
2 tablespoons chopped parsley

Sieve flour and salt into a bowl and rub in fats till the mixture resembles fine breadcrumbs. Add sufficient water to mix to a pliable dough. Wrap and chill for 30 minutes if possible. Roll out pastry and use to line a 20 cm (8 in) flan ring or 4 10 cm (4 in) patty tins. Lay crab meat in the bottom and sprinkle with onion. Beat eggs together with salt, pepper, cayenne and milk, then beat in cream and parsley. Pour into flan and cook at 220°C (425°F, Gas 7) for 20 minutes then reduce heat to 180°F (350°F, Gas 4) and continue cooking for about 25 minutes for a large flan and 15 minutes for small flans, till set firm and golden brown. Serve hot or cold.

SPRATS

This small silvery fish of the herring family, rich in oil, is available fresh and sometimes smoked. The fish is eaten whole like whitebait; allow 200 g ($\frac{1}{2}$ lb) per person. Clean well and draw through the gills, wipe dry and dip in seasoned flour. Thread onto skewers and grill under a moderate heat until browned and cooked through, turning once. Serve very hot with lemon and/or mustard sauce and brown bread and butter. When smoked sprats are available serve as part of an hors d'oeuvre or by themselves. Delicious with lemon.

SQUID WITH TOMATOES

Squid is a comparatively new catch for the Scottish boats, but many are now being landed in the Moray Firth and exported to the Mediterranean.

600 g ($1\frac{1}{2}$ lb) squid
2 tablespoons oil
1 large onion, peeled and chopped
1 clove garlic, crushed
300 g ($\frac{3}{4}$ lb) tomatoes, skinned and chopped (or use canned tomatoes)
1 tablespoon tomato paste
125 ml ($\frac{1}{4}$ pint) red or white wine
Salt and black pepper
1–2 teaspoons sugar
Pinch of paprika
Chopped parsley for garnish

To prepare the squid: pull the head away from the bag, and from inside the bag discard the nib-like piece of hard transparency called the 'pen'. Remove the purplish-red veil of skin from the body. Wash well inside and out. Cut the body into rings, and the edible veil-like fins and tentacles into 2 cm (approx 1 in) pieces. Dry well. In the soft part of the head find the long narrow ink sac, the dark colour showing through a transparent skin. Keep aside. Discard the head and soft entrails. Heat the oil in a pan and fry the squid, onion and garlic till lightly browned. Add tomatoes, tomato paste and wine, and season lightly. Crush the ink sac, mix with a little water and strain into the pan. Simmer uncovered for 15–20 minutes till the squid is tender and the sauce is thick. Adjust seasonings, add sugar and paprika to taste, and serve sprinkled with parsley.

SCAMPI IN WHISKY

2 large onions, peeled and
 chopped
1 clove garlic, crushed (optional)
1 tablespoon oil
75 g (3 oz) butter
1 tablespoon flour
125 ml (¼ pint) dry white wine
125 ml (¼ pint) fish stock or light
 chicken stock
Salt and pepper
4–8 tablespoons double (heavy)
 cream
400 g (1 lb) scampi
4 tablespoons whisky

Sauté onions and garlic gently in oil and 25 g (1 oz) butter till soft but not coloured. Stir in the flour and cook for 1 minute. Add wine and stock, bring to the boil and simmer gently for 10 minutes. Season well then stir in the cream. Melt remaining butter in a pan and toss the scampi in it for a few minutes. Warm whisky, set it alight and pour over scampi, turning them till the flames disappear. Add the sauce and bring just up to the boil. Serve in a ring of creamed potatoes or boiled rice.

SCOTCH WOODCOCK

Small can anchovy fillets, drained
60 g (2½ oz) butter
4 slices toast
4 eggs, beaten
Salt and pepper
3 tablespoons milk or single
 (light) cream
1 tablespoon chopped parsley

Chop half the anchovy fillets and blend with 40 g (1½ oz) butter. Spread over the toast and keep warm. Beat eggs with seasonings and milk or cream. Melt the remaining butter in a pan and add the egg mixture. Cook gently, stirring frequently, till creamy and scrambled. Stir in parsley then spoon over the toast. Garnish with remaining anchovy fillets and serve immediately.

SAUCES

Tartare Sauce

125 ml (¼ pint) thick mayonnaise
1 tablespoon lemon juice
1–3 teaspoons vinegar
1 tablespoon chopped gherkins
1–2 tablespoons chopped capers
1–2 tablespoons chopped parsley
1–2 teaspoons chopped chives
 (optional)
½ teaspoon finely chopped onion
 (optional)

Mix all the ingredients together in a bowl and leave to stand for at least 30 minutes for flavours to blend before serving.

Hollandaise Sauce

2 tablespoons wine or tarragon
   vinegar
1 tablespoon water
2 egg yolks
100 g (4 oz) butter
Salt and pepper
Lemon juice

Place the vinegar and water in a small pan and boil until reduced by 1 tablespoon. Put egg yolks into a basin or the top of a double saucepan and stir in the vinegar. Put over a pan of gently simmering water and cook gently, stirring all the time, until the mixture thickens. Whisk in butter, a small piece at a time, then season to taste. If the sauce is too bland, add a little lemon juice; if it is too sharp, add more butter. Serve warm.

MEAT

Some hae meat and canna eat,
And some wad eat that want it;
But we hae meat, and we can eat,
And sae the Lord be thanket.

Robert Burns, 'The Selkirk Grace' (so called because when Burns was visiting the Earl 'of Selkirk on St Mary's Isle, he was asked to say grace, and responded with these famous lines).

It has been said that a nation cannot afford to eat meat on an agricultural economy; although this idea has been disproved by the high standard of, for example, the New Zealand and Australian agricultural economies, the Scottish Highland fat stock farmer has long been dependent on the prosperous, densely populated south of Scotland and England to provide an outlet for his superb beef. His Aberdeen Angus bulls, of course, have been sold all over the world to help build up and strengthen other stocks.

The beef export business south from the north of Scotland was based mainly on the best cuts — roasts, fillets and other steaks — resulting in the local inhabitants eating the very best of what have come to be known as the cheaper cuts. Mince, in cattle-rearing areas of Scotland, is top quality beef, not poor fatty leftovers as in some places. Mince and tatties make a real dinner. And while the economy made the use of offal a distinct necessity, the gastronomic merits of tongue, liver, kidney, lights, tripe, sweetbreads and the rest have always been appreciated by the Scots.

The haggis, which was originally a good, cheap, country meal, has been elevated in some quarters to a ceremonial dish, sometimes eaten with whisky poured over it. This is unfortunate. Haggis should be as popular an everyday dish as the sausage, and to pour whisky over it is, in my opinion, spoiling good haggis and wasting good whisky. Let's put haggis back on the family table! It's much easier to buy it ready-made from quality butchers or delicatessens, or canned, than to make it oneself — it's rather an unpleasant job and the ingredients are not always available; a recipe has been included here mainly for the benefit of readers in those countries that do not permit the import of haggis.

HAGGIS

1 sheep's bag
Sheep's pluck (liver, lights, heart)
100 g ($\frac{1}{4}$ lb) suet
4 medium onions, peeled and
   blanched
200 g ($\frac{1}{2}$ lb) pinhead (coarse) oatmeal, lightly toasted
2–4 tablespoons salt
1 teaspoon black pepper
1 teaspoon powdered mixed
   herbs

Wash the bag in cold water, scrape it carefully and clean well. Soak in cold water overnight. Wash the pluck and place in a pan with the wind pipe hanging out into a basin to catch any drips. Cover with water and boil gently for 2 hours. Leave to cool in the cooking liquor overnight. Grate the liver, and chop the heart, lights and suet with the onions, and mix with the oatmeal, salt, pepper, herbs and 500 ml (1 pint) pluck liquor. Mix well, and use to fill the bag just over half full. Sew up securely (but not tightly) for the oatmeal swells, and cook in a pan of gently boiling water for 3 hours, pricking the bag occasionally to prevent bursting. Remove from the pan and serve with 'neeps and tatties' (see next recipe), or cool and reheat when required.

Note: The bag can be cut into 2 or 3 smaller pieces to make smaller haggis, in which case boil for $1\frac{1}{2}$–2 hours.

HAGGIS FLAN

23 cm (9 in) cooked pastry flan
   case
400 g (1 lb) neeps (swedes),
   peeled and diced
50 g (2 oz) butter
Salt and pepper
1 canned haggis
400 g (1 lb) creamy 'chappet
   tatties' (mashed potatoes)

Place the prepared flan on a baking sheet (or make the case using 150 g/6 oz shortcrust pastry, see p. 97) and bake blind at 220°C (425°F, Gas 7) for 10 minutes, then reduce to 180°C (350°F, Gas 4) for a further 10–15 minutes. Cook neeps in boiling salted water till tender. Mash well and beat in 40 g ($1\frac{1}{2}$ oz) butter and plenty of salt and black pepper. Spread over the base of the flan case. Heat the haggis and put a layer over the neeps. Finally cover with a layer of mashed potatoes and fork the top. Dot with the remaining butter and cook at 190°C (375°F, Gas 5) for about 30 minutes, finishing off under the grill if necessary to give a browned top. Serves 6.

POWSOWDIE (SHEEP'S HEAD BROTH)

The sheep's head should be cleaned by the butcher who will skin it and remove the eyes and brains.

1 sheep's head, split
3 litres (6 pints) water
100 g (4 oz) pearl barley
Salt and black pepper
200 g (½ lb) onions, peeled and
    chopped
1 leek, cleaned and chopped
200 g (½ lb) turnips, peeled and
    chopped
200 g (½ lb) carrots, peeled and
    chopped
Bouquet garni (see p. 3)
2 tablespoons fine oatmeal
Chopped parsley

Wash the head thoroughly and soak overnight in cold water. Put head in a pan, cover with cold water, bring to the boil then strain. Soak the brains in cold water if to be used. Clean head thoroughly then return it to pan with 3 litres (6 pints) water and the barley. Bring slowly to the boil and remove scum. Add seasoning and simmer for 1½–2 hours. Add vegetables and bouquet garni and simmer for a further 2 hours. Add chopped brains (optional) and oatmeal and simmer for 30 minutes. Adjust seasonings, remove bouquet garni and serve sprinkled with parsley. Serves 10–12.

Note: The head can be served in the soup, separately with a sauce or in a ragout.

POTTED HEAD

Many butchers in Scotland sell this ready-cooked. If you buy it, note that it does not always freeze well. The quantities given in this recipe are large, but Potted Head has always sold particularly well at charity sales.

1 ox head, split
2 tablespoons salt
2 small onions
2 tablespoons peppercorns
4 blades of mace
1 teaspoon allspice
4 sprigs each of thyme, mar-
    joram and parsley
4 bay leaves
8 cloves

After soaking the head for a few hours, scald it, then scrape well when cool. Put it in a large pan, cover well with cold water, add salt, bring to the boil slowly, and remove scum. Simmer for 5–6 hours, then remove and take off meat from the head. Return the bones to the liquor, adding water to cover if necessary. Add all the herbs and spices and simmer for 2 hours more. Take the lid off the pan and boil rapidly to make the stock jellify when cool. Strain into a basin, leave to get cold, then remove the fat from the top of the jellied stock. Cut the meat into small pieces and place in wetted moulds or basins. Warm the stock to melt it, and when cool pour into the moulds. Stir to distribute the meat, and leave to get cold. When set, turn out and garnish with parsley. A good-sized head will make about 7.25 kg (16 lb).

Note: If the stock does not jellify, add gelatine — approx 20 g (½–¾ oz) gelatine to 500 ml (1 pint) liquid — to the stock when warming it to put into the moulds, making sure it dissolves.

SHEPHERD'S PIE

There have been more sheep than people in Scotland for a very long time. The large sheep population of Scotland and the popularity of mutton and lamb made Shepherd's Pie a popular dish, especially since it was made from the remains of the meat, carved off the joint. Similarly, the remains of a beef joint and the Scottish housewife's unwillingness to throw anything away made Cottage Pie popular: but both must be made from cooked meat. Shepherd's Pie or Cottage Pie made with fresh minced meat is a second-rate substitute.

12 g ($\frac{1}{2}$ oz) dripping or margarine
1 large onion, peeled and chopped
1 clove garlic, crushed (optional)
1 teaspoon flour
Approx 125 ml ($\frac{1}{4}$ pint) stock or gravy
1–2 tablespoons tomato ketchup (catsup)
1 teaspoon Worcestershire sauce
Salt and pepper
200 g (8 oz) cooked lamb, minced (ground)
1 tablespoon chopped parsley or 1 teaspoon mixed herbs
400 g (1 lb) cooked potatoes, mashed

Melt dripping or margarine in a pan, and fry onion and garlic if used till golden brown. Stir in flour, followed by enough stock to moisten thoroughly. Add ketchup, sauce and seasoning, then stir in meat and herbs and mix well. Turn into a heatproof dish and cover with a layer of mashed potato. Mark the top of the potato with a fork or the blade of a knife, and cook at 200°C (400°F, Gas 6) for about 30 minutes till the top is evenly browned. Serve hot.

Note: To make Cottage Pie used cooked minced beef. Other additions such as a can of tomatoes, haricot beans or peas can be added to either pie.

ROAST LAMB

Leg or shoulder of lamb
Salt and pepper
Little dripping
2 cloves garlic, crushed
2 teaspoons dried rosemary

Weigh joint, then wipe and sprinkle with salt and pepper. Place in a roasting tin with a little dripping. Lightly score the skin of the meat and rub crushed garlic into the cuts. Sprinkle with rosemary and cook at 220°C (425°F, Gas 7), allowing 25 minutes per 400 g (1 lb) plus 20 minutes over. (For a really thick or rolled joint allow 30 minutes per 400 g (1 lb) plus 20 minutes over.) Baste two or three times during cooking, and use pan drippings to make gravy with meat or vegetable stock.

POT ROAST LAMB

2–3 large breasts of lamb, boned
4 lean rashers bacon, derinded
Fresh sage or thyme leaves
Salt and pepper
25 g (1 oz) dripping
250 ml (½ pint) stock or water
2 large onions, peeled and sliced
3 carrots, peeled and sliced
2 sticks celery, sliced

Remove excess fat from lamb, lay bacon and sage or thyme over it and season lightly. Roll the meat up tightly and secure with string and skewers. Melt dripping in a heavy saucepan or frying pan and brown the meat all over. Either leave in pan or transfer to a large casserole. Add stock, cover and either simmer or cook at 150°C (300°F, Gas 2) for about 1 hour. Add vegetables and continue to cook for another hour or till tender. Strain vegetables and serve separately from the meat. Remove fat from the cooking liquor, adding more stock if necessary, adjust seasonings and serve as a thin gravy. Serves 4–6.

BOILED MUTTON WITH CAPER SAUCE

1½–2 kg (3½–4½ lb) leg of mutton
2 large onions, peeled and sliced
2 large carrots, peeled and sliced
Bouquet garni (see p. 3)
1 turnip, peeled and chopped
  (optional)
Sprig of fresh rosemary (optional)
Salt and pepper
50 g (2 oz) butter
50 g (2 oz) flour
250 ml (½ pint) milk
1–2 tablespoons capers
2 teaspoons caper liquor or
  vinegar

Trim the joint, removing any excess fat, and weigh. Place in a large saucepan with the onions, carrots, bouquet garni, turnip and rosemary if used, and seasonings. Add water to barely cover the joint, and bring to the boil. Remove scum, cover and simmer till tender, allowing 25–30 minutes per 400 g (1 lb) plus 25 minutes over. Remove meat and keep warm. Skim fat off the cooking liquor and reserve 250 ml (½ pint). Melt butter in pan. Stir in flour and cook for 2 minutes. Gradually add the milk and reserved cooking liquor and bring to the boil, stirring frequently. Add capers and liquor and season well. Simmer for 3 minutes and serve with the meat. If the sauce is too thick, add a little more cooking liquor. Serves 6.

Note: Instead of all water to cook the meat in, a mixture of milk and water can be used. Use the remaining liquor for the base of soup once the fat has been removed. If capers are not available, dried nasturtium seeds can be used.

Top: Roast Partridge (p. 61) with game chips and gravy.

Bottom: Game Pie (p. 67), Roast Pheasant (p. 62) and Bread Sauce (p. 57).

CAULD DAY BEEF CASSEROLE

4 pieces braising steak, 125 g
    (5 oz) each
Salt and pepper
2 tablespoons dripping or oil
1 large onion, peeled and
    chopped
2 tablespoons flour
500 ml (1 pint) stock
2 leeks, cleaned and sliced
4 sticks celery, sliced
4 carrots, peeled and cut into
    sticks
1 bayleaf
Dumplings (see p. 5)

Season beef, place in a pan and brown all over in the melted dripping. Transfer to a casserole. Fry onion in the same fat then stir in the flour and cook for 1–2 minutes. Add stock and bring to the boil. Add leeks, celery, carrots and bayleaf, season well and pour into the casserole. Cover and cook at 160°C (325°F, Gas 3) for about 1¾ hours till tender. Meanwhile make dumplings and cook separately in gently boiling water for 15 minutes. Drain. Remove the bayleaf from the casserole, adjust seasonings, and top with dumplings.

Note: Before the introduction of the casserole and the modern gas and electric ovens, this recipe was made as a stew in a thick-bottomed, shallow iron pan.

RICH BEEF STEW

500 g (1¼ lb) chuck steak, cubed
Seasoned flour
1 tablespoon dripping or oil
1 large onion, peeled and sliced
2 sticks celery, sliced
250 ml (½ pint) beef stock
125 ml (¼ pint) red wine
Salt and pepper
1 bayleaf
100 g (4 oz) button mushrooms

Coat meat in seasoned flour then brown in hot fat. Remove to a casserole. Add onions and celery to the fat and fry gently till soft. Add stock and wine, seasoning and bayleaf and bring to the boil. Pour over the meat or return meat to the saucepan. Cover casserole and cook at 160°C (325°F, Gas 3) for 1½–2 hours till tender, or simmer gently in the saucepan for about 1½ hours till tender (adding a little more stock if necessary). Add mushrooms 15 minutes before the stew is ready. The liquor can be thickened with a little cornflour (cornstarch) blended in cold water, if liked. Adjust seasonings and serve.

BOILED BEEF AND CARROTS

1–1.5 kg (2½–3½ lb) joint of salt
    silverside or brisket
4–8 carrots, peeled and thickly
    sliced
6–8 small onions, peeled and
    thickly sliced
1–2 turnips, peeled and quartered
4 parsnips, peeled and quartered
1 bayleaf
Black pepper

Place joint in a saucepan with the other ingredients and add enough water just to cover. Bring to the boil slowly, skim and cover. Simmer gently for about 2–2½ hours till meat is tender. Remove bayleaf, strain off liquor for gravy and serve meat on carving plate with vegetables in a side dish. Serves 6.

Roast Venison (p. 68) with roast potatoes, gravy and Brussels sprouts.

MINCE

12 g (½ oz) dripping or margarine
400 g (1 lb) minced (ground)
   beef
1 onion or 2 shallots, peeled and
   quartered
Salt and pepper
2 tablespoons hot water or gravy

Melt fat in a pan and add the mince and onion or shallots. Beat well to remove all the lumps then heat gently, stirring frequently till all the pink colour has disappeared. Add salt and pepper to taste, and water or gravy. Cover and simmer very gently for about 40 minutes till tender, stirring occasionally. Adjust seasonings and serve. Serves 3–4.

Note: If you buy your steak from the butcher have it minced before your very eyes as was and is the custom in Scotland. The mincing machines in the Scottish butchers' shops are usually in the front of the shop and not hidden in the back, as is very often the case elsewhere.

SAVOURY MINCE

25 g (1 oz) dripping or margarine
1 onion or 2 shallots, peeled and
   thinly sliced
1 clove garlic (optional)
400 g (1 lb) minced (ground)
   beef
200 g (8 oz) can peeled tomatoes
Salt and black pepper
1 teaspoon Worcestershire sauce
Little stock or water
100 g (4 oz) mushrooms, chopped
½ green pepper, deseeded and
   sliced (optional)

Melt fat in a pan. Fry onion or shallots, and garlic if used, till soft and beginning to brown. Add mince and cook gently for about 5 minutes, stirring frequently. Add tomatoes, salt, pepper and Worcestershire sauce and bring to the boil. Add a little stock, if necessary. Turn into a heatproof dish, cover and cook at 160°C (325°F, Gas 3) for about 40 minutes. Add mushrooms and green pepper if used. Stir well, cover and return to the oven for a further 15 minutes.

POT ROAST OF BEEF

1.25–1.75 kg (3–4 lb) joint
    topside or brisket of beef
Salt and pepper
1 tablespoon dripping or oil
1 onion, peeled and quartered
4–6 cloves
250 ml (½ pint) stock or water

Season meat. Heat dripping in a heavy saucepan and brown meat all over. Either leave in pan to cook over a low heat or transfer to a large casserole. Add onion and cloves to the pan with the stock and either cover and simmer very gently, turning joint several times, for about 3 hours till tender, or cover and cook at 150°C (300°F, Gas 2) for 3 hours or until tender. Extra vegetables such as sliced carrots, turnips, parsnips and leeks can be added to the pan after 2 hours' cooking. Serve the meat and vegetables separately. Make gravy from the juices in the pan (after fat is removed) and vegetable stock which can be thickened with cornflour (cornstarch) if preferred. Serves 6.

ROAST BEEF

This is very much a 'special day' dish. I specifically do not refer to it as a 'Sunday' dish as it was not unusual for a Scottish housewife to serve a cold lunch on Sunday. The tradition of keeping the Sabbath as a day of rest plus the fact that, in most homes, the whole family went to Church at 11 o'clock in the morning, reduced the facilities for serving a hot midday meal.

Joint of sirloin, ribs, rump,
    topside, etc
Salt and pepper
Little dripping
6–12 shallots, peeled (optional)
3–4 parsnips, peeled and par-
    boiled (optional)

Weigh joint and wipe over. Season with salt and pepper and place in a roasting tin with a little dripping. Arrange vegetables around the joint. Cook at 220°C (425°F, Gas 7), allowing 20 minutes per 400 g (1 lb) plus 20 minutes over for a joint on the bone, and 23–25 minutes per 400 g (1 lb) plus 20 minutes over for a thickly rolled joint. Beef should be served still pink in the middle; for really rare beef cook for about 15 minutes less than the suggested times. Baste two or three times during cooking. Use pan drippings to make gravy with meat or vegetable stock. Serve with horseradish cream or sauce.

BEANS WITH BACON

The absence of pork recipes in this book is accounted for by the fact that pork was never very popular in Scotland — one writer has gone as far as to say that after the Reformation and the extensive reading of the Old Testament well into the nineteenth century, devout Scots may have, to some extent, subconsciously become inured with Jewish diet laws. The reluctance to eat certain types of fish and shellfish could suggest that there is more than speculation involved here.

In spite of this, bacon has always been popular but invariably cut very thin; the canny Scot again perhaps, but it does taste better.

200 g (8 oz) haricot or butter beans
200 g (8 oz) streaky bacon rashers, derinded and chopped
1 onion, peeled and finely chopped
12 g (½ oz) butter or dripping
Black pepper
Salt
200 g (8 oz) can peeled tomatoes (optional)
1 tablespoon chopped chives or chopped parsley

Soak beans in cold water overnight then drain thoroughly. Fry the bacon and onion in butter or dripping till beginning to brown then toss in the beans and continue to fry gently till the bacon is browned and beans heated through. Add tomatoes if required, cover and simmer gently for 5–10 minutes. Serve hot sprinkled with chives or parsley. Serves 3–4.

FRIED BACON ROLLS

300 g (12 oz) collar bacon, de-rinded
1 onion, peeled
50 g (2 oz) fresh breadcrumbs
Black pepper
½ teaspoon ground nutmeg
1 tablespoon chopped parsley
Salt
1 egg, beaten
Little seasoned flour
Dripping or oil for frying
2 tomatoes

Mince (grind) the bacon and onion then mix with breadcrumbs, pepper, nutmeg, parsley and a little salt if necessary. Bind together with egg and divide into 4. Shape into round flat cakes and coat in seasoned flour. Fry gently in dripping or oil till golden brown (about 7–8 minutes) then turn and continue on the other side till cooked through and well browned. Drain on absorbent paper and serve with a slice of tomato.

Note: For a change serve with a fried or poached egg.

200 g (½ lb) bacon rashers (streaky
   or collar), derinded and
   chopped
400 g (1 lb) mashed potatoes
1 tablespoon chopped parsley
1 tablespoon finely chopped
   onion
Salt and pepper
1 egg, beaten
Little flour
Golden crumbs or raspings

800 g (2 lb) best end of neck of
   mutton or lamb
1 tablespoon dripping or oil
2 large onions, peeled and thickly
   sliced
1 turnip, peeled and diced
3–4 carrots, peeled and sliced
1 bayleaf
Salt and pepper
100 g (4 oz) haricot beans, soaked
   overnight (or use canned
   variety)
2 teaspoons mushroom ketchup
   (catsup)
2 tablespoons chopped parsley

100 g (4 oz) streaky bacon rashers,
   derinded and chopped
1 large onion, peeled and sliced
8 slices lamb's liver, approx
   400 g (1 lb)
Little seasoned flour
1 tablespoon dripping or oil
1 red pepper, deseeded and sliced
375 g (15 oz) can peeled tomatoes
125 ml (¼ pint) stock or water
Salt and black pepper
1 teaspoon dried marjoram

BACON AND POTATO CROQUETTES

Fry the bacon quickly in its own fat till crispy then
drain well and add to the mashed potato with parsley,
onion and seasonings. Mix well and add a little of the
beaten egg to bind. Divide into 8 and form into
barrels. Dip first in flour then into the beaten egg and
finally in the crumbs. Heat shallow fat in a pan and
fry the barrels for about 10 minutes, turning carefully
till well browned. Drain on absorbent paper and serve
hot with a vegetable or salad. Serves 3–4.

HARICOT HOTPOT

Cut the meat into neat chops. Melt dripping in a
large pan and add meat. Fry for a few minutes,
turning frequently till beginning to brown. Add
onions, turnip and carrots and continue to fry for
about 3 minutes. Add sufficient water to just cover the
meat, the bayleaf, plenty of seasonings and the drained
beans. Bring to the boil, remove scum, cover and
simmer very gently for about 2 hours till tender, or
transfer to a covered casserole and cook at 160°C
(325°F, Gas 3) for about 2½ hours. Remove bayleaf,
stir in ketchup and parsley and adjust seasonings before
serving.

BRAISED LIVER

Fry bacon and onion in a pan till well browned.
Transfer to a casserole. Dip liver in seasoned flour and
fry in the dripping in the pan till sealed all over.
Place on top of bacon and onions. Add red pepper to
pan and fry for a few minutes then add tomatoes,
stock or water, seasoning and marjoram. Bring to the
boil, pour over liver and cover casserole. Cook at
180°C (350°F, Gas 4) for about 45 minutes till tender.

43

BOILED TONGUE

1 pickled ox tongue
1 carrot, peeled and sliced
1 onion, peeled and sliced
2 sticks celery, sliced
Bouquet garni (see p. 3)

Wash and trim tongue then soak in cold water for 2–3 hours. Tie into a round with string or skewers and place in a large pan with all the other ingredients and add sufficient water to just cover. Bring to the boil, skim, and cover the pan. Simmer very gently for about 3–4 hours till tender. Plunge the tongue into cold water and quickly remove skin, any bones and gristle. To serve cold, put into a convenient-sized round cake tin, cover with a saucer and a weight and leave to get cold. Turn out and serve with salad. To eat hot, cut into slices and serve with a parsley or tomato sauce garnished with lemon wedges.

TRIPE AND BACON ROLLS

400 g (1 lb) dressed tripe
8 rashers bacon, derinded
1 onion, peeled and finely chopped
Salt and pepper
2 tablespoons chopped parsley
250 ml ($\frac{1}{2}$ pint) stock or water
125 ml ($\frac{1}{4}$ pint) milk
1 tablespoon cornflour (cornstarch)
4 tomatoes, halved
Sprigs of parsley

Cut tripe into strips about 8 cm (3 in) wide and cover each with rashers of bacon. Sprinkle with onion, seasoning and parsley then roll each up and secure with fine string, cotton or cocktail sticks. Place in a casserole and pour boiling stock or water over the rolls. Cover and cook at 180°C (350°F, Gas 4) for about 1½ hours. Strain off liquor and make up to 375 ml ($\frac{3}{4}$ pint) with milk. Thicken with cornflour blended in a little cold water and simmer for 3 minutes. Adjust seasonings, pour back over tripe and serve with grilled tomatoes and parsley for garnish.

TRIPE AND ONIONS

400 g (1 lb) dressed tripe
4 large onions, peeled and chopped
500 ml (1 pint) milk
1 bayleaf
Salt and pepper
25 g (1 oz) butter
25 g (1 oz) flour
1 teaspoon lemon juice

Cut tripe into 5 cm (2 in) pieces and place in a pan with the onions, milk, bayleaf and seasonings. Bring to the boil, cover and simmer gently for about 2 hours till tender, or place in a covered casserole and cook at 160°C (325°F, Gas 3) for about 2½ hours. Strain off liquor. Melt butter in a pan, stir in flour, and cook for 1 minute. Gradually add strained liquor and bring to the boil, stirring frequently. Season to taste, add lemon juice and return tripe and onions to the pan. Reheat and serve with boiled potatoes.

MEAT LOAF

300 g (12 oz) cooked beef or raw
    stewing steak
100 g (4 oz) smoked streaky
    bacon rashers, derinded
1 onion, peeled
1 clove garlic, crushed (optional)
75 g (3 oz) fresh white bread-
    crumbs
1 teaspoon Worcestershire sauce
2 tablespoons tomato ketchup
    (catsup)
1 tablespoon chopped parsley
Salt and pepper
1 egg, beaten
Watercress
Gherkins
1 hardboiled egg, sliced

Mince (grind) beef, bacon, onion, and garlic if used, and mix in breadcrumbs, Worcestershire sauce, ketchup, parsley, salt and pepper to taste. Bind with egg and pack into a lightly greased small loaf tin or basin. Cover with greaseproof paper and then tightly enclose in foil. Place in a steamer or saucepan with boiling water to come halfway up the basin and simmer for 1½–2 hours. Leave to cool in the pan then weight and chill. Turn out and garnish with watercress, gherkins, and sliced hardboiled egg. Serves 4–6.

SWEETBREADS

400 g (1 lb) prepared lamb's or
    sheep's sweetbreads (see note
    below)
1 small onion or 2 small shallots,
    peeled and chopped
2 carrots, peeled and chopped
2 sticks celery, chopped
Bouquet garni (see p. 3)
2 teaspoons lemon juice
Salt and pepper
Stock or water
40 g (1½ oz) butter or margarine
40 g (1½ oz) flour
125 ml (¼ pint) milk
4 tablespoons single (light) cream
Chopped parsley

Place sweetbreads in a pan with the onion or shallots, carrots, celery, bouquet garni, 1 teaspoon lemon juice and seasoning, and just cover with stock or water. Bring to the boil, remove scum, cover and simmer gently for about 1 hour till tender. Strain off the liquor and reserve 250 ml (½ pint). Keep sweetbreads warm. Melt butter or margarine in a pan, stir in the flour and cook for 1 minute. Gradually add the cooking liquor, milk and remaining lemon juice and bring to the boil. Season to taste and return sweetbreads and vegetables to the sauce. Bring back to the boil, stir in the cream and pour into a warmed dish. Serve sprinkled with parsley.

Note: To prepare sweetbreads, first wash them very well then soak in cold water for 1 hour. Drain and put into a pan with cold water to cover, a pinch of salt and squeeze of lemon juice. Bring to the boil, and simmer for 5 minutes, drain, and immediately plunge into cold water. Wash thoroughly again and remove any fat, skin or tubes.

FRIED SWEETBREADS

400 g (1 lb) prepared lamb's or
    sheep's sweetbreads
Little seasoned flour
1–2 eggs, beaten
Golden breadcrumbs or raspings
6–8 rashers streaky bacon, de-
    rinded
Little dripping or oil for frying
Parsley sprigs

Prepare sweetbreads, if not already done (see previous recipe for method), dry on absorbent paper and cut into thick slices. Dip first in seasoned flour then into beaten egg and finally in breadcrumbs, pressing these well into to give a good coating. Cut bacon rashers into long strips. Melt a little dripping in a pan and fry bacon till golden brown. Drain and keep warm. Fry coated sweetbreads in the same fat till golden brown, turning several times. Drain on absorbent paper and serve very hot garnished with fresh or fried parsley and a tartare or tomato sauce.

KIDNEY AND BACON

6–8 lambs' kidneys, approx 400 g
    (1 lb)
1 large onion or 3–4 shallots,
    peeled and chopped
100 g (4 oz) streaky bacon, de-
    rinded and chopped
1 tablespoon dripping
2 teaspoons flour
250 ml ($\frac{1}{2}$ pint) stock
Salt and pepper
$\frac{1}{4}$ teaspoon grated lemon rind
1 tablespoon lemon juice

Halve kidneys and remove skins and cores. Cut each piece in half again. Fry the onion or shallots and bacon in dripping till beginning to brown, then add kidneys and continue to cook for 3–4 minutes till well sealed. Stir in flour then gradually add the stock. Bring to the boil, season well, and add lemon juice. Cover and simmer gently for 10–15 minutes till tender. Adjust seasonings and serve.

FRIED STEAKS

4 pieces or rump, sirloin or fillet
Salt and pepper
25 g (1 oz) butter
1 tablespoon oil
125 ml ($\frac{1}{4}$ pint) red wine or stock
1 tablespoon finely chopped
    onion or shallot
Watercress for garnish

Season steaks with salt and pepper. Heat butter and oil in a pan and, when hot, add the steaks. Fry for 3–5 minutes each side till browned on the outside: the time depends on whether rare or well-cooked steaks are required. Remove to a plate and keep warm. Add wine, onion or shallot, and seasonings to the pan, bring to the boil and pour over steaks. Garnish with watercress and serve at once.

Note: Alternatively, fry 2 large sliced onions in the pan before frying the steaks and place on top of them when cooked, making the sauce without the addition of chopped onion. Skirlie (see p. 78) is also a good accompaniment.

DORNIE BARRELS

200 g (½ lb) cooked leftover meat
50 g (2 oz) shredded suet
100 g (4 oz) cooked rice
60 g (2½ oz) fresh breadcrumbs
Salt and pepper
Good pinch of ground nutmeg
    or mace
1 egg, beaten
1–2 tablespoons milk
Fat or dripping for frying

Chop meat finely or mince (grind) it, mix with suet, rice, breadcrumbs, salt, pepper and nutmeg or mace, and bind together with the egg and milk. Divide into 6–8 pieces and form into barrel shapes. Fry in shallow fat for about 10 minutes, turning frequently till browned all over and cooked through. Serve hot with grilled tomatoes and oatcakes. Serves 3–4.

CASSEROLE OF HEARTS

3–4 lambs' hearts, trimmed
1 tablespoon dripping or oil
8–12 shallots or button onions,
    peeled
4 carrots, peeled and quartered
200 g (½ lb) swede, peeled and
    diced
2 leeks, cleaned and sliced
4 tomatoes, sliced
500 ml (1 pint) beef stock or
    water
Salt and pepper
1 tablespoon cornflour (corn-
    starch)

Cut hearts into thick slices or quarters, removing all tubes. Heat dripping or oil in a pan and brown the meat all over. Transfer to a casserole. Fry shallots or onions in the same oil and add to the casserole with the carrots, swede, leeks and tomatoes. Add stock and seasoning, cover and cook at 160°C (325°F, Gas 3) for 2–2½ hours till tender. Blend cornflour with a little water, stir into casserole and return to the oven for 5 minutes. Adjust seasonings and serve.

HIGHLAND HOTPOT

600 g (1½ lb) neck of lamb
1–2 lamb's kidneys, skinned,
    cored and chopped
2 large onions, peeled and sliced
2 large carrots, peeled and
    chopped
400 g (1 lb) potatoes, peeled and
    sliced
250 ml (½ pint) stock
Salt and pepper
Good pinch of ground nutmeg
1 teaspoon Worcestershire sauce
12 g (½ oz) dripping or margarine

Cut lamb into pieces and layer up in a casserole with the kidneys, onions, carrots and potatoes, finishing with a layer of potatoes. Season stock well with salt, pepper, nutmeg and Worcestershire sauce and pour into the casserole. Dot potato with softened dripping or margarine, cover and cook at 160°C (325°F, Gas 3) for about 2 hours till tender. Remove lid, turn oven to 220°C (425°F, Gas 7) and continue to cook for about 20 minutes till potatoes are brown.

COTTER'S HOTPOT

400 g (1 lb) shin of beef
200 g (½ lb) skinless pork chipolatas
Little seasoned flour
400 g (1 lb) potatoes, peeled and
 sliced
1 large cooking apple, peeled,
 cored and sliced
2 large onions, peeled and sliced
4 tomatoes, peeled and sliced
Salt and pepper
375 ml (¾ pint) beef stock
Pinch of ground nutmeg
½–1 teaspoon Worcestershire
 sauce

Trim meat and cut into small cubes, and cut each chipolata into three pieces, then dip both in seasoned flour. Arrange in layers with the potatoes, apple, onions and tomatoes, starting and ending with a layer of potato. Season the stock well with salt, pepper and nutmeg, add Worcestershire sauce and pour into casserole. Cover and cook at 180°C (350F°, Gas 4) for 1½ hours then remove lid, add a little more stock if necessary and continue to cook uncovered for ½–1 hour till tender.

SAUSAGE ROLLS

300 g (¾ lb) puff pastry (chilled
 or frozen)
400 g (1 lb) beef sausagemeat
1 small onion, peeled and finely
 chopped
1 tablespoon chopped parsley
 (optional)
Beaten egg to glaze

If using frozen pastry, thaw it out. Combine sausage-meat, onion, and parsley if used, and divide mixture into two. Roll out pastry to a rectangle about 50×30 cm (20×12 in) and cut in half lengthwise to give two long strips. Roll each piece of sausagemeat to a roll the same length as the pastry and place on it just to one side of the centre. Brush the edge with the beaten egg and fold the pastry over to enclose filling. Press edges well together and neaten with a knife. Brush top with beaten egg and cut into 3 cm (1½ in) pieces. Place on a damp baking sheet, make two cuts in the top of each roll and cook at 200°C (400°F, Gas 6) for about 20 minutes till golden brown. Serve hot or cold. Makes about 20.

Note: Pork sausagemeat or a combination of sausage-meat and bacon or salami can be used in place of beef sausagemeat. If you want to make the puff pastry yourself, see the basic recipe on p. 97.

SCOTCH MUTTON PIES

Mutton pies were, and are still, eaten at every opportunity in Scotland. They are the 'pie and a pint' pie in Scotland, heated behind the bar in a pub. They can also be bought hot in cafés of all types, very often with cooked dried peas soaked overnight and, if available, thick brown gravy. The pie to a Scotsman anywhere is a mutton pie. They are made fresh every day by the bakers, sold to pubs and cafés and bought extensively by the housewives and hotted up under the grill or in the oven.

Filling

12 g (½ oz) dripping or fat
300 g (12 oz) breast of mutton or lamb, minced (ground)
1 small onion or 2 shallots, peeled and minced
Approx 125 ml (¼ pint) stock or water
Salt and black pepper
1 teaspoon chopped parsley
1–2 teaspoons Worcestershire sauce
25 g (1 oz) fresh breadcrumbs (optional)

Pastry

110 g (4½ oz) blended lard (shortening)
125 ml (¼ pint) water
300 g (12 oz) plain flour
¾ teaspoon salt
Little beaten egg or milk

Melt fat in a pan and add meat and onion or shallots. Cook very slowly, stirring frequently, for a few minutes till sealed. Add a little stock to moisten, cover and simmer gently for 10 minutes. Stir in salt and pepper to taste, parsley, Worcestershire sauce and breadcrumbs and leave to cool.

Make hot water crust pastry by melting the fat in the water and bring to the boil. Add to the flour and salt and mix to a soft dough. Knead lightly and cover the bowl to keep the dough warm. Divide two-thirds of the dough into 6 and roll each piece out to line a deep 8 cm (3 in) tin or ring tin, or mould it round the base of a tumbler. Fill cases with the meat mixture, moistening with a little stock if necessary. Cover with lids made from remaining pastry, damping the edges and pressing well together. Trim with scissors if necessary, make a hole in the centre of each pie for steam to escape and stand on a baking sheet. Cook at 200°C (400°F, Gas 6) for about 25 minutes then remove and brush with egg or milk, making sure that the centre hole is not blocked. Return to the oven at 180°C (350°F, Gas 4) for about ¾ hour till cooked through. Remove pies from tins and fill up with stock through the centre hole if necessary. Always serve hot. Makes 6.

FORFAR BRIDIES

Bridies are made and sold mainly in and around the county of Angus and are available on similar lines to the mutton pies in the previous recipe. They are smaller but contain much more meat than the well-known Cornish Pasty or 'tiddy oggy'.

200 g (½ lb) plain flour
Pinch of salt
50 g (2 oz) margarine
50 g (2 oz) lard
Water
200 g (½ lb) stewing steak, minced (ground) or chopped
25 g (1 oz) shredded suet
Salt and pepper
1 onion, peeled and minced
1 teaspoon Worcestershire sauce
Good pinch of ground nutmeg

Sieve flour and salt into a bowl, rub in fats till mixture resembles fine breadcrumbs, then add sufficient cold water to mix to a stiff dough. Knead lightly, cover and put to rest in a cool place for at least 10 minutes. Combine minced steak, suet, seasonings, onion, Worcestershire sauce, and nutmeg. Roll out pastry and cut into 4 15 cm (6 in) rounds or ovals. Place meat mixture on one side of each piece of pastry, damp edges and fold over to enclose the filling like a pasty. Press edges well together and crimp. Place on a dampened baking sheet and make a small hole in the top of each for steam to escape. Cook at 200 °C (400°F, Gas 6) for 20 minutes then reduce heat to 180°C (350°F, Gas 4) and continue for a further 25–35 minutes till meat is cooked through. Serve hot or cold.

Note: Originally Forfar Bridies were made with a flour and water paste but it tended to get very hard during cooking and now shortcrust or puff pastry (see p. 97) gives a better result. If best steak is used it is not necessary to mince it; just cut thinly, beat well and cut into thin strips.

POULTRY

The hen has always played an important part in the Scottish agricultural economy. The farmer's wife always got the hen and egg money, and in many cases it was her only source of income, replacing the more traditional housekeeping money system operating in most homes. It would seem likely that vigilant tax gatherers and more prosperous farmers have put an end to this method of paying the 'wife'.

The cockerels in the flock and the old hens past laying provided the family with good food. The bird was usually boiled, thus providing two courses — soup and poultry. Visitors were often treated to a hen, and this is the basis of the story that on one farm where quite a lot of entertaining was done, the hens, which normally scratched round the back door, ran and hid whenever a visitor arrived as they knew one of them was for the pot.

BOILED HEN

1–1.5 kg (2½–3½ lb) boiling fowl
or 4 chicken portions
Few pieces leftover ham or
bacon
Bouquet garni (see p. 3)
2 sticks celery, chopped
1 large onion, peeled and sliced
Salt and pepper
1 litre (2 pints) water

Wash the fowl well and place in a large pan with the ham, bouquet garni, celery, onion, seasonings and water. Bring to the boil, remove scum, cover and simmer gently for 1½–2 hours till tender.

Note: The traditional Scottish stuffing for boiling hen is oatmeal and onion (see p. 56). Alternatively, as a time saver, mealie puddings (see p. 80) are placed in the cavity.

HOWTODIE

1.5–2 kg (3½–4 lb) oven-ready
  chicken
75 g (3 oz) butter
6 button onions or shallots,
  peeled
Good pinch of ground mace
2 cloves
500 ml (1 pint) boiling stock
  (made from giblets)
800 g (2 lb) spinach, prepared
Chicken liver, finely chopped
2–4 tablespoons double (heavy)
  cream

Stuffing

50 g (2 oz) fresh breadcrumbs
Little milk
1 shallot or ½ onion, peeled and
  finely chopped
1 teaspoon dried tarragon
1 teaspoon chopped parsley
Salt and pepper

To make the stuffing, soak breadcrumbs in a little milk until pulpy then add onion or shallot, tarragon and parsley and season well. Mix together and use to stuff neck end of bird, securing the opening with a skewer or string.

Melt butter in a heatproof casserole and brown the onions or shallots. Place chicken in the casserole and coat with the melted butter. Cook at 200°C (400°F, Gas 6) for about 20 minutes till browned then add mace, cloves, seasonings and stock to the pan. Cover casserole and return to the oven at 180°C (350°F, Gas 4) for 50–60 minutes till tender. Meanwhile cook spinach in boiling salted water and drain very well. Keep hot. Remove bird from the oven and strain stock into a pan. Keep chicken hot. Add liver to the stock and simmer gently for 5 minutes, then mash into the stock. Add cream, adjust seasonings and reheat without boiling. Place chicken on a hot serving dish and arrange spinach around it. Pour sauce over the chicken only, and serve at once. Serves 6.

Note: Traditionally Howtodie was served with 'Drappit Eggs'. To do this, poach one egg per person in the stock before adding the liver, remove and serve on the spinach around the chicken.

STOVED CHICKEN

1.25–1.5 kg (2½–3 lb) oven-ready
  roasting chicken
50 g (2 oz) butter
1 tablespoon oil
Approx 1 kg (2½ lb) potatoes,
  peeled and sliced
16 shallots, peeled, or 2 large
  onions, peeled and sliced
Salt and pepper
500 ml (1 pint) stock (made from
  giblets)
3 tablespoons freshly chopped
  parsley

Cut chicken into eight pieces and brown in 25 g (1 oz) butter and the oil heated together. Using a large heavy casserole, layer up potatoes, onions or shallots and chicken, seasoning well between layers and finishing with a layer of potatoes. Pour over the boiling stock, then dot with remaining butter. Cover with a piece of greaseproof paper, then the lid. Cook at 140°C (275°F, Gas 1) for 2½–3 hours till tender. Add a little more boiling stock if necessary during cooking. Sprinkle with parsley and serve.

POT ROAST CHICKEN

1.25–1.5 kg (3–3½ lb) oven-ready
   chicken
100 g (4 oz) sausagemeat
Salt and pepper
1 small onion, peeled and
   chopped
2 tablespoons chopped parsley
25 g (1 oz) fresh breadcrumbs
Little grated lemon rind
50 g (2 oz) butter
200 g (8 oz) lean bacon, derinded
   and cubed
12 button onions or 2 large
   onions, peeled and quartered
400 g (1 lb) potatoes
150 g (6 oz) button mushrooms
Lemon wedges for garnish

Wipe chicken inside and out. Combine sausagemeat, seasonings, onion, parsley, breadcrumbs and lemon rind and use to stuff neck end of chicken. Secure and truss bird. Brown the chicken carefully all over in the melted butter then transfer to a large casserole. Brown bacon and onions in the same fat then add to the chicken, pouring the fat over it. Season, cover and cook at 180°C (350°F, Gas 4) for about 30 minutes. Meanwhile peel potatoes, cut into 2.5 cm (1 in) dice and boil for 2–3 minutes in salted water. Drain and add them to the casserole, basting with the fat, and return to the oven for 1 hour. Add mushrooms and continue for a further 20–30 minutes till chicken is tender. Serve on a carving plate garnished with lemon and the vegetables and juices straight from the casserole. Serves 4–6.

ROAST CHICKEN

Wipe inside and outside of bird and stuff the neck end (see stuffings, p. 56). Do not stuff too tightly or use too dry a mixture or the skin will probably burst during cooking. Chickens can be cooked unstuffed in which case it is better to place a knob of butter a quartered onion, or a few slices of lemon inside to g flavour. Weigh the trussed chicken and place in a roasting tin. Brush all over with melted butter or oil and sprinkle with salt and pepper fatty bacon can be laid over the breast, at 220°C (425°F, Gas 7), allowing 20 minutes per 400 g (lb) plus 10 minutes, basting occasionally and covering with a piece of greaseproof paper or foil if it is getting too brown. Alternatively wrap chicken loosely in foil, place in a roasting tin and cook at the same temperature but increase cooking time by 5–10 minutes and fold back foil for last 15–20 minutes for bird to brown up. It can also be cooked in a transparent roasting bag or film following the maker's instructions. Serve with roast potatoes, bread sauce, thin gravy made from pan drippings and giblet stock, bacon rolls and a green vegetable.

SUNDAY CHICKEN

1.25 kg (3 lb) oven-ready boiling
   chicken
2 onions, peeled and chopped
1 bayleaf
Salt and pepper
2 carrots, peeled and sliced
Juice of ½ lemon
50 g (2 oz) butter
50 g (2 oz) flour
100 g (4 oz) button mushrooms,
   quartered
4–6 tablespoons double (heavy)
   cream
4–8 rashers streaky bacon, rolled
   and cooked
Triangles of toast
Chopped parsley

Place chicken, onions, bayleaf, seasonings, carrots and lemon juice in a pan with sufficient water to just cover chicken. Bring to the boil, cover and simmer very gently for about 1 hour till tender. Giblets can also be added to the pan or used in other stock. Remove chicken and take off the skin. Cut the flesh into cubes or strips. Melt butter in a pan, stir in the flour and cook for 1 minute. Gradually add 500 ml (1 pint) strained cooking liquor and bring to the boil. Season well, add chicken meat, mushrooms and some of the vegetables strained from the stock and simmer for 5–10 minutes. Stir in cream and reheat without boiling. Pour into a dish and garnish with cooked bacon rolls, small triangles of toast and chopped parsley. Serves 4–5.

Note: For a change, add 50 g (2 oz) grated cheese, or 4 skinned, deseeded and chopped tomatoes, or 2 tablespoons sherry to the sauce just before serving. The chicken bones can be returned to the cooking liquor with more water to make soup.

ROAST TURKEY

A male (stag) turkey is called a 'bubbly jock' in Scotland.

Wipe the bird inside and out and then stuff (see p. 56), truss and weigh. Cover all over with a layer of softened butter, sprinkle with salt and pepper and lay streaky bacon rashers all over the breast. Cook either at 160°C (325°F, Gas 3), in which case foil is not necessary except to protect the legs during cooking and to prevent the breast getting too brown; or at 230°C (450°F, Gas 8), when the whole bird must be wrapped completely in foil before being put into the roasting tin. The foil is folded back for the last 20–30 minutes of cooking time to brown up, if necessary.

Serve roast turkey with bread sauce and/or cranberry sauce or jelly, bacon rolls, chipolatas, roast potatoes, a green vegetable, and gravy made from the pan drippings and giblet stock.

Highland Potato Cakes (p. 73), Stovies (p. 74), Scotch Eggs (p. 75) and Baked Eggs (p. 74).

ROAST DUCK

Although ducks look large and meaty there is more fat on them than on a chicken and very little flesh attached to the bones; therefore allow 340–400 g (rather less than 1 lb) oven-ready weight per person. Always look for a young bird — as with all poultry and game, older birds get much tougher. Signs of a young bird are the yellow bill and feet and the ease with which the webbing between the feet can be torn. With age the yellow turns darker and becomes quite red.

Pluck and draw as for all poultry. Young ducks do not need stuffing, unless preferred, but an older bird is improved with a good sage and onion stuffing or an orange and apricot flavoured stuffing. Always stuff at the tail end of duck then truss, but don't pull the wings across the back as for chicken. Prick skin all over with a fine skewer to allow excess fat to escape during cooking, and sprinkle with salt and pepper. Stand in a roasting tin without any fat and cook at 200°C (400°F, Gas 6), allowing 15 minutes per 400 g (lb) plus 15 minutes. Baste once or twice during cooking. Duck can be stood on a rack in the roasting tin so that all fat is kept away from the bird. If this is done, baste at least twice during cooking. Serve with apple sauce, a thin gravy made from pan drippings and giblet stock, new potatoes, peas and orange salad.

A GOOD DUCK RECIPE

2.5 kg (5 lb) duck
Salt and pepper
3 oranges
1 lemon
1 tablespoon sugar
1 tablespoon vinegar
2 tablespoons brandy (or water)
2–3 teaspoons cornflour (cornstarch)

Place trussed duck on a rack or in a roasting tin, prick skin, season with salt and pepper, and cook at 200°C (400°F, Gas 6), allowing 15 minutes per 400 g (lb) plus 15 minutes, till tender. Meanwhile thinly pare rind from 1 orange and cut into thin strips. Cook in boiling water for 5 minutes then drain. Squeeze juice from all oranges and lemon. Melt sugar in a small pan with the vinegar and heat to make a dark brown caramel. Add brandy or water, orange and lemon juice, and simmer gently for 2–3 minutes. Remove duck to a serving dish and keep warm. Pour excess fat from roasting tin and add orange sauce to the pan drippings. Thicken with cornflour blended in a little water. Add orange rind strips and simmer for 3–4 minutes. Adjust seasonings and serve separately with the duck and with an orange and watercress salad.

Beetroot in Arrowroot (p. 71), Potato Omelette (p. 73), Tattie Scones on a girdle (p. 92) and Kilted Kippers (p. 16).

ROAST STUFFED GOOSE

3.5 kg (8 lb) oven-ready goose
2 onions, peeled and finely
   chopped or minced
2 teaspoons dried sage
1 orange
150 g (6 oz) fresh breadcrumbs
1 tablespoon chopped parsley
Salt and pepper
1 egg, beaten

Wipe the goose thoroughly. Remove giblets and use to make stock. Mix together onion, sage, orange rind and flesh, breadcrumbs, parsley and seasonings, bind together with the egg and use to stuff tail end of bird. Truss the goose and stand on a rack in a roasting tin. Sprinkle skin with salt and rub in. Lay a double sheet of greaseproof paper over the goose without tucking into the tin. The feet can be wrapped in foil to prevent burning. Cook at 200°C (400°F, Gas 6), allowing 15 minutes per 400 g (lb) and 15 minutes over. Baste the goose only once, after cooking for 1 hour. Remove paper for the last 20 minutes to brown up the skin. Serve with a gooseberry or sour apple sauce and a gravy made from the pan drippings and giblet stock. Serves 6–8.

Note: Allow approx 400 g ($\frac{3}{4}$–1 lb) oven weight of goose per person.

STUFFINGS FOR CHICKEN AND TURKEY

Note: When stuffing the neck end of a turkey, use double the amount of stuffing (except for chestnut stuffing).

Oatmeal and Onion Stuffing

200 g (8 oz) medium oatmeal
200 g (8 oz) shredded suet
1 large onion or 6 shallots, peeled
   and chopped
Salt and black pepper

Toast the oatmeal lightly under the grill or in a moderate oven. Mix with the suet, onion or shallots and plenty of salt and pepper. Do not add any liquid to bind together.

Apricot Stuffing

375 g (15 oz) can apricot halves *or*
   100 g (4 oz) dried apricots,
   soaked
75 g (3 oz) fresh breadcrumbs
$\frac{1}{2}$ medium onion, grated
Salt and pepper
1 tablespoon chopped parsley
Lemon juice
50 g (2 oz) chopped walnuts
   (optional)
25 g (1 oz) butter
1 egg, beaten

Drain and chop apricots (use the juice from the canned apricots in the sauce or gravy for a change). Mix with breadcrumbs, onion, salt and pepper, parsley, a good squeeze of lemon juice, and the chopped walnuts if used. Bind together with the butter and beaten egg.

Bread Sauce

4–6 whole cloves
1 medium onion
375 ml ($\frac{3}{4}$ pint) milk
Salt and pepper
Small bayleaf (optional)
75 g (3 oz) fresh breadcrumbs
Approx 20 g ($\frac{1}{2}$–1 oz) butter

Stick the cloves into the onion and place in a saucepan with the seasoned milk and the bayleaf if used. Bring slowly just up to the boil and leave to infuse for at least 20 minutes. Remove the bayleaf and add breadcrumbs. Mix well and cook slowly for about 10 minutes, stirring frequently. Remove the onion, adjust seasonings, beat in the butter and serve hot.

Celery and Apple Stuffing (also use for duck and goose)

50 g (2 oz) bacon, chopped
3 sticks celery, finely chopped
1 large onion, peeled and chopped
25 g (1 oz) butter or dripping
Approx 70 g (2–3 oz) fresh breadcrumbs
2 tablespoons chopped parsley
Salt and pepper
$\frac{1}{2}$ teaspoon sugar
2 cooking apples, peeled, cored and finely chopped
A little lemon juice

Fry bacon, celery and onion in the butter or dripping till beginning to colour. Mix in breadcrumbs, parsley, salt and pepper, sugar and apples. Bind together with a little lemon juice and more melted butter, if necessary.

Chestnut Stuffing (for turkey only)

50 g (2 oz) bacon, chopped
1 teaspoon chopped parsley
Grated rind of $\frac{1}{2}$–1 lemon
Salt and pepper
100 g (4 oz) fresh breadcrumbs
200 g (8 oz) chestnut puree (either canned or freshly boiled and sieved)
25 g (1 oz) melted butter
Beaten egg

Fry bacon in its own fat till browned then mix with parsley, grated lemon rind, salt and pepper, breadcrumbs and chestnut puree. Bind together with the butter and a little beaten egg.

Salami Stuffing

1 onion, chopped
25 g (1 oz) butter
60 g (2½ oz) fresh breadcrumbs
2 tablespoons chopped parsley
½ teaspoon dried thyme
¼–½ teaspoon finely grated
   orange rind
Salt and pepper
50 g (2 oz) salami, finely chopped
1 egg, beaten

Fry orange in butter till soft then add breadcrumbs, parsley, thyme, orange rind, salt and pepper and salami. Bind together with the beaten egg.

Veal Forcemeat

100 g (4 oz) lean stewing veal
Approx 100 g (3–4 oz) lean
   bacon
1 onion, peeled
75 g (3 oz) fresh breadcrumbs
50 g (2 oz) mushrooms, chopped
2 teaspoons chopped parsley
Salt and pepper
Good pinch of ground mace
1 egg, beaten

Finely mince (grind) veal with bacon and onion. Mix with breadcrumbs, mushrooms, parsley, salt, pepper and mace. Bind together with the beaten egg.

GAME

From the twelfth of August, 'The Glorious Twelfth', it is legally permissible to shoot grouse until the close of the season at the end of January.

Although the wood pigeon, as distinct from the 'street' or 'kirk-steeple' pigeon, is not officially classed as game, it is included in this section as it has always had a special place in Scotland. Feeding off the crops, the pigeon in the 'doocot' (dovecote) provided fresh meat in winter, before the introduction of the turnip made it possible for the farmer to feed beef animals through the winter.

Rabbits are not officially classed as game either, but shooting rights are closely guarded by the lairds and farmers, and wild rabbits contributed greatly to the Scottish agricultural economy.

After many years of small coveys (for which the use of the combine harvester was blamed) partridges are now once more plentiful in Scotland.

Game has only become readily available in towns since the big shooting estates, for economic reasons, started selling their game commercially. Before this, much of the 'bag' was presented to the local guests and tenantry. Limited supplies came from poachers, but the penalties were high (and the fines are still considerable). Deep freezing has also helped to preserve the large quantities of game shot over a limited period.

ROASTING GAME BIRDS

All young birds are served at their best when roasted, but as they lack fat, it is necessary to lard the breast with a piece of fat or fatty bacon and place a knob of seasoned butter in the cavity before cooking. During cooking all game should be basted frequently. It is better to braise or casserole older birds as they tend to become tough with age. All game birds need to be hung by the neck immediately after shooting and before being plucked, otherwise the flesh will be dry, tough and tasteless. The length of time depends both on individual taste and the type of weather. For the average taste the bird is ready to eat when the tail or breast feathers can be plucked easily — usually 7–10 days. All birds are plucked before eating but some are not drawn. Snipe and woodcock have the entrails left in and should not be hung for more than a few days; they should then be cooked on toast as for Roast Grouse (see p. 63). Truss all game as for poultry but do not remove feet or pull the sinews. Larger game birds can sometimes be jointed before cooking or split along the back and flattened.

PIGEON WITH WHISKY

2 large or 4 small pigeons,
  plucked and drawn
Salt and pepper
25 g (1 oz) butter
1 tablespoon oil
4 shallots or 1 large onion, peeled
  and finely chopped
100 g (4 oz) mushrooms, chopped
3 tablespoons whisky
125 ml ($\frac{1}{4}$ pint) dry white wine
125 ml ($\frac{1}{4}$ pint) stock
1 tablespoon lemon juice
Pinch of cayenne pepper
4 tablespoons double (heavy)
  cream
Chopped parsley

Divide each pigeon in half and remove backbone. Season well with salt and pepper. Heat butter and oil in a pan and brown pigeons all over. Remove and keep warm. Fry onions or shallots and mushrooms till soft then return pigeons to the pan. Pour on the warmed whisky and set alight. Add wine, stock, seasoning, and lemon juice and bring to the boil. Cover and simmer very gently for about 30 minutes till tender (add more stock if necessary). Adjust seasonings and add cayenne. Just before serving stir in the cream and sprinkle with parsley.

CASSEROLE OF PIGEON

4 large pigeons, plucked and
  drawn
1 orange, quartered
8 rashers streaky bacon
1 tablespoon oil
25 g (1 oz) butter
1 large onion, peeled and
  chopped
1 tablespoon flour
125 ml ($\frac{1}{4}$ pint) marsala or red
  wine
250 ml ($\frac{1}{2}$ pint) stock
100 g (4 oz) button mushrooms
4 juniper berries (optional)
Salt and pepper

Insert a piece of orange in each pigeon, lay 2 rashers of bacon over each bird and truss. Heat oil and butter in a pan and brown the birds all over. Transfer to a large casserole. Fry onion in same fat till beginning to brown then stir in flour and cook for 1 minute. Gradually add marsala or red wine and stock and bring to the boil. Add mushrooms and juniper berries if used, season to taste and pour over pigeons. Cover tightly and cook at 190°C (375°F, Gas 5) for about 1$\frac{1}{2}$ hours till tender.

DOOCOT PIE (PIGEON PIE)

2 large pigeons, plucked and
   drawn, halved
100 g (4 oz) braising steak, diced
Little seasoned flour
Dripping or oil for frying
1 bayleaf
$\frac{1}{4}$ teaspoon dried thyme
$\frac{1}{2}$ small onion, peeled and
   chopped
Salt and pepper
Chicken stock or gravy
200 g ($\frac{1}{2}$ lb) puff pastry (see p. 97)
Beaten egg for glazing

Toss pigeons and steak in seasoned flour then fry in a little dripping till well browned. Transfer to a pie dish. Sprinkle with crushed bayleaf, thyme, onion, salt and pepper then add sufficient stock to half fill the dish. Roll out pastry thinly and use to cover pie dish, decorating top with the trimmings. Make a hole in the centre for steam to escape. Brush with beaten egg and cook at 220°C (425°F, Gas 7) for about 20 minutes then reduce heat to 180°C (350°F, Gas 4) and continue for 1–1$\frac{1}{4}$ hours till meat is tender. Cover pie with foil or greaseproof paper to prevent browning.

ROAST PARTRIDGE

All partridges should be hung for 3–6 days but only very young birds are suitable for roasting. Young birds have pointed wing feathers and yellowish legs, but with age the feathers become rounded and legs turn bluish-grey.

Season trussed bird inside and out and place a knob of butter in the cavity. Cover breasts with pieces of pork fat or bacon fat, tying lightly in position if necessary. Place birds in a baking tin with hot dripping and cook at 230°C (450°F, Gas 8) for 10 minutes then reduce to 200°C (400°F, Gas 6) for 15–30 minutes depending on size, basting frequently. Remove pieces of fat about 5 minutes before serving to brown up the breasts. Serve on circles of fried bread with a thin gravy made from the pan drippings (orange-flavoured for a change), bread sauce or cranberry sauce, game chips and a celery and apple or green salad. Allow one partridge per person, though very large birds may serve two portions.

Note: A buttered vine leaf can be placed on the breast under the bacon for a variation in flavour. It also prevents the breast drying out whilst the legs are still cooking.

ROAST PHEASANT

Pheasant should be hung for at least one week after shooting, but some people will leave it for over two weeks to get really high before plucking and drawing. The time will depend on the mildness of the weather. Wipe the trussed bird inside and out and put a knob of butter and a little lemon juice in the cavity. Cover breast with slices of fatty bacon, stand in a roasting tin with a little hot dripping and cook at 220°C (425°F, Gas 7) for 45–70 minutes depending on size, basting frequently. The bacon can be removed 15 minutes before the end of cooking and the breast dredged with flour. Serve with fried crumbs, bread sauce, game chips and thin gravy made from the pan drippings. Garnish with watercress and orange or lemon slices. Serves 3–5 depending on size.

PHEASANT CASSEROLE

1 large pheasant
Seasoned flour
Dripping for frying
4 rashers streaky bacon, derinded and chopped
150 g (4–6 oz) mushrooms, sliced
1 bayleaf
Approx 375 ml ($\frac{3}{4}$ pint) stock
2 tablespoons port or red wine (optional)
Chopped parsley

Joint pheasant and coat in seasoned flour. Brown in the melted dripping then place in a casserole with the bacon, mushrooms and bayleaf. Add salt and pepper and sufficient stock to half cover the pheasant. Add port or red wine if used, cover and cook at 180°C (350°F, Gas 4) for about 1 hour or till tender. Adjust seasonings, remove bayleaf, and serve sprinkled with parsley.

Note: This is an excellent way of cooking old cock pheasants which tend to be tough when served roasted.

DUKE'S PHEASANT

1 large plump pheasant or a brace of pheasants
Approx 80 g (2–4 oz) butter
600 g (1$\frac{1}{2}$ lb) cooking apples
Grated rind of $\frac{1}{2}$ lemon
Salt and black pepper
125 ml ($\frac{1}{4}$ pint) single (light) cream
Watercress

Prepare and truss the bird(s). Melt 25 g (1 oz) butter in a pan and brown the pheasant all over. Peel, core and thickly slice the apples and place half in a roasting tin or casserole. Sprinkle with lemon rind and place the pheasant on top. Arrange remaining apples around the bird. Melt the remaining butter and pour over. Season with salt and pepper. Spoon cream over the apples and cover dish with foil or a lid. Cook at 180°C (350°F, Gas 4) for 1–1$\frac{1}{2}$ hours till tender. Arrange on a serving dish garnished with watercress.

SHOOTING LODGE GROUSE

2 young grouse
50 g (2 oz) melted butter
Salt and pepper
100 g (4 oz) fresh breadcrumbs
  (brown or white)
Paprika pepper
8 rashers streaky bacon, derinded
4 tomatoes, halved
Game chips
Lemon wedges
Watercress

Slit grouse down the back and flatten. Brush flesh side liberally with melted butter and season lightly. Place either in a grill pan or in a roasting tin and grill under moderate heat for 5–10 minutes or cook at 220°C (425°F, Gas 7) for 10 minutes. Sprinkle liberally with crumbs and lightly with paprika and continue to grill for about 20 minutes or return to the oven for 25–30 minutes till cooked through. Meanwhile make bacon into rolls and grill or bake with the tomatoes alongside the grouse. Serve garnished with game chips, lemon wedges, watercress and a thin gravy made from the pan drippings.

Note: Pheasant and partridge can also be cooked in this way, partridge needing rather less cooking and pheasant rather more.

ROAST GROUSE

Grouse should be hung for at least 3 days, and preferably 5 or 6 depending on the weather, before plucking and drawing. Season trussed bird inside and out and place a knob of seasoned butter in the cavity. Cover breast with a piece of pork fat or fat bacon and stand on a piece of toast in a roasting tin. Cook at 200°C (400°F, Gas 6) for about 30–45 minutes, basting frequently during cooking. Remove fat or bacon after 20 minutes' cooking and dredge breast with flour. Serve grouse on the toast on which it was cooked with a thin gravy, matchstick potatoes, fried crumbs and bread sauce. A watercress or lettuce salad is a good accompaniment. Serves 2–3.

Note: Grouse can be roasted without toast for the first 20 minutes then placed on toast when the bacon is removed. The toast absorbs all the delicious juices from the bird.

  Ptarmigan, which turns white in the winter, is often called white grouse, and blackcock is known as black grouse. Both are rather scarce, but can be cooked as for grouse.

RABBIT AND HARE

Rabbit

Both wild and specially bred rabbits are eaten. Fresh and frozen rabbits are usually sold ready skinned and cleaned, but watch out for a bluish tinge on fresh rabbits for this is a sign of staleness. As soon as possible after killing, rabbits should be hung by the hind legs for 2 to 3 days and preferably paunched. Before cooking, they should be well washed and soaked in salted, cold water.

Hare

Similar to a rabbit but much larger with a darker flesh and richer flavour. Hare should be hung by the hind feet without paunching for about a week with a bowl under the nose to catch the blood (used for thickening in Jugged Hare, see p. 66). Most hares are sold ready paunched and often jointed and you can sometimes get the blood as well. However, with frozen hares it is not possible to retain it.

STEWED RABBIT

1 rabbit, jointed
375 ml ($\frac{3}{4}$ pint) stock or water
1 onion, peeled and sliced
$\frac{1}{4}$ teaspoon grated lemon rind
1 bayleaf
Salt and pepper
50 g (2 oz) butter
50 g (2 oz) flour
250 ml ($\frac{1}{2}$ pint) milk
8 rashers streaky bacon, derinded
  and rolled

Soak rabbit in cold, salted water for 30–60 minutes then drain. Put stock in a pan with the onion, lemon rind, bayleaf and seasonings, bring to the boil and add the rabbit. Cover and simmer gently for about 1½ hours till tender. Remove rabbit to a warm, deep dish. Strain off 250 ml ($\frac{1}{2}$ pint) cooking liquor. Melt butter in a pan and stir in flour. Cook for 1 minute then gradually add the measured liquor and the milk, stirring frequently. Simmer for 3 minutes and season well. Pour over the rabbit and serve very hot garnished with grilled or fried bacon rolls.

RABBIT PIE

1 young rabbit, approx 800 g (2 lb), jointed
200 g ($\frac{1}{2}$ lb) collar bacon in a piece, derinded and chopped
375 ml ($\frac{3}{4}$ pint) stock or water
1–2 onions, peeled and sliced
2 carrots, peeled and sliced
1 bayleaf
Juice of $\frac{1}{2}$ lemon
Salt and pepper
25 g (1 oz) flour
1–2 tablespoons freshly chopped parsley
150 g (6 oz) shortcrust pastry (see p. 97)
Beaten egg or milk for glazing

Soak rabbit in cold, salted water for at least 2 hours then drain well. Place in a pan with the bacon, stock or water, onions, carrots, bayleaf, lemon juice and seasonings. Bring to the boil, cover and simmer for 45–60 minutes till tender. Strain off liquor and thicken with flour blended in a little cold water. Return to the boil, stirring frequently, adjust seasonings and add parsley. Remove rabbit from the bones and return the meat, cooked ham and vegetables to the sauce. Pour into a pie dish and leave to cool. Roll out pastry larger than top of dish and cut a 2 cm (1 in) strip for the rim of the dish. Dampen rim, position pastry strip then dampen it. Cover with pastry lid, press edges firmly together and crimp. Decorate with leaves from pastry trimmings. Brush with egg or milk and cook at 200°C (400°F, Gas 6) for 20 minutes then reduce to 180°C (350°F, Gas 4) for a further 15–20 minutes. Serves 4–6.

Note: This can be made into a double crust pie and served hot or cold or covered with puff pastry (see p. 97) instead of shortcrust.

RABBIT IN BEER

25 g (1 oz) butter
1 tablespoon oil
1 rabbit, jointed
Seasoned flour
150 g (6 oz) collar bacon, derinded and diced
1 onion, peeled and sliced
Approx 350 ml ($\frac{1}{2}$–$\frac{3}{4}$ pint) light ale
1 teaspoon sugar
1 teaspoon vinegar
Bouquet garni (see p. 3)
12 soaked prunes (optional)
1–2 teaspoons French mustard

Heat the butter and oil in a flameproof casserole. Coat rabbit in seasoned flour and fry in the fat till well browned. Remove rabbit. Brown bacon and onion in the same fat then return rabbit to the pan. Add ale a little at a time and bring to the boil. Add sugar, vinegar, seasonings and bouquet garni, cover and simmer very gently for about 1 hour till tender, or cover and cook at 180°C (350°F, Gas 4) for 1 hour. Add prunes if used, stir in mustard and continue to simmer for 10 minutes. Adjust seasonings and serve.

JUGGED HARE

125 ml (¼ pint) red wine
4 tablespoons oil
½ teaspoon marjoram
1 onion, peeled and sliced
2 bayleaves
Pinch of ground cloves
Salt and pepper
1 hare, skinned and jointed
2 carrots, peeled and sliced
2 sticks celery, sliced
Bouquet garni (see p. 3)
Grated rind and juice of 1 small
    orange
500 ml (1 pint) beef stock
25 g (1 oz) cornflour (cornstarch)
1 tablespoon redcurrant jelly
4 tablespoons port
Hare's blood

Place wine, 2 tablespoons oil, marjoram, onion, bayleaves, cloves and seasonings in a bowl, add hare and marinate for 12–24 hours, turning several times. Remove hare and fry in remaining oil till well browned and transfer to a casserole. Wipe out pan, add marinade, carrots, celery, bouquet garni, orange rind and juice, stock and seasonings to the pan, bring to the boil and pour over hare. Cover tightly and cook at 160°C (325°F, Gas 3) for about 3½ hours till tender. Strain off liquor and thicken with cornflour blended in a little water, return to the boil and adjust seasonings. Stir in redcurrant jelly, port and blood. Reheat without boiling and pour back over hare. Serves 4–8 depending on size of hare.

HIGHLAND HARE CAKES

1 onion, peeled and finely
    chopped
25 g (1 oz) butter
200 g (8 oz) boneless hare (cooked
    or raw)
150 g (6 oz) belly pork, skinned
50 g (2 oz) stale bread
Little milk or water
Salt and pepper
½ teaspoon celery salt
¼ teaspoon paprika pepper
1 tablespoon mushroom ketchup
    (catsup) or 1 teaspoon
    Worcestershire sauce
1 egg, beaten
Golden crumbs or raspings
Savoury butter (see recipe)

Fry onion in butter till soft but not coloured. Mince (grind) the hare and pork and mix thoroughly. Soak bread in milk or water until soft then squeeze out. Add bread to the meat with onion, salt, pepper, celery salt, paprika, and ketchup or Worcestershire sauce. Mix well and bind with the egg. Divide into 8 and shape into flat cakes. Coat thoroughly in crumbs and fry gently in hot shallow fat for about 10 minutes each side till golden brown and cooked through. Serve topped with a pat of savoury butter, made by creaming 50 g (2 oz) butter with salt, pepper, a little lemon juice and 1 tablespoon of finely chopped parsley, and chilled until required.

Note: This is a good way of using leftover hare or venison from soup-making or any other dish.

ROAST WILD DUCK

All types of wild duck should hang for 2–3 days only before plucking and drawing as the flesh tends to turn sour if kept too long. Truss like a domestic duck, season well inside and out and rub all over with softened butter to prevent drying out. Place in a roasting tin and cook at 220°C (425°F, Gas 7), allowing 40–50 minutes for wild duck, 25–30 minutes for teal, 20–40 minutes for pintail and widgeon, and baste frequently. Do not overcook or the bird will lose flavour and become very dry and unappetizing. Halfway through cooking, pour a little orange juice (fresh or canned), port or burgundy over the bird to bring out the flavour. Serve with thin gravy or orange or wine sauce made from the pan drippings, and an orange salad or watercress and orange or lemon wedges.

Note: Mallard serves 3–5; widgeon and pintail serve 2; teal serves ½–1.

GAME PIE

200 g (½ lb) stewing veal
200 g (½ lb) cooked bacon or ham
½ small onion, peeled
Salt and pepper
Good pinch of ground mace
1 cooked pheasant or a mixture of cooked and boned game, approx 250 g (10 oz)
125 g (5 oz) lard (shortening)
125 ml (¼ pint) water
300 g (12 oz) flour
¾ teaspoon salt
1 egg, beaten
2 teaspoons powdered gelatine
250 ml (½ pint) stock made from game bones

Mince (grind) the veal, bacon and onion, add salt, pepper and mace and mix well. Chop meat from the pheasant. Make hot water pastry by melting fat in the water and bring to the boil. Add to the flour and salt and mix to a soft dough. Knead lightly on a board then roll three-quarters of the pastry into a 24 cm (9½ in) round. Carefully lower into a 16 cm (6½ in) loose-bottomed round cake tin or a game pie mould and press lightly to line it evenly. Put three-quarters of the minced meats around the edges of the pie, place chopped game in the middle and then cover with remaining minced meats. Roll out the rest of the pastry for a lid, moisten edges with beaten egg and position. Press edges well together, trim, and crimp. Make a hole in the centre of the lid and decorate with leaves from pastry trimmings. Cook at 200°C (400°F, Gas 6) for 30 minutes then brush with beaten egg. Reduce heat to 160°C (325°F, Gas 3) and continue for 1½ hours, covering with foil as it gets brown. Dissolve gelatine in the hot stock, cool then pour into pie through central hole. When cold fill up with more stock. Chill till firm. Remove from tin and serve with salads. Serves 6–8.

ROAST VENISON

Young animals should be hung at least one week and older, tougher animals a fortnight or more, so that they become slightly high and the flavour is at its best. Wipe down occasionally with a cloth to remove moisture. Test at intervals by running a skewer through the haunch; when a faint 'high' smell is apparent, the venison is ready for cooking. The best joints for roasting are the saddle for a large joint, or a fillet from the saddle, the haunch or loin for a smaller one. It is usual to marinate venison before cooking as it tends to be very dry.

Marinade

2 onions, peeled and chopped
2 carrots, peeled and chopped
2 sticks celery, chopped
Freshly ground black pepper
Few parsley stalks ⎱
1 bayleaf ⎬ *
2–3 blades mace ⎰
Red wine or water
*or bouquet garni (see p. 3)

Place everything except the wine or water in a container large enough to take the venison and then add sufficient wine or water to half cover it. Leave to marinate for 8–12 hours turning 2–3 times. Remove meat and drain well then brush liberally with oil. Loosely package in foil, stand in roasting tin and cook at 160°C (325°F, Gas 3), allowing 25–30 minutes per 400 g (lb). Fold back foil 20 minutes before the end of the cooking time, baste well, then dredge with flour and return to the oven to brown up. Serve hot with a thick gravy made from the pan drippings, and cranberry, rowan or redcurrant jelly.

Note: Before foil was available, it was traditional to cover the meat in a paste made by mixing flour and water to stiff dough and rolling it out to 1 cm ($\frac{1}{2}$ in) thickness.

VEGETABLES AND EGGS

IF YOU CAN'T BUY IT, GROW IT

No doubt there will be readers of this book who for one reason or another will be unable to buy some of the vegetables — and fruit — used in the recipes in this book. Why not try to grow them? Your local seedsmen or nurserymen can give advice about suitable growing conditions for whatever part of the world you live in. If certain plants and seeds are not available, readers should contact one of the following:

Alexander and Brown (Seedsmen)
Perth
Scotland

William Smith and Sons Ltd (Seedsmen)
Hazelhead
Aberdeen
Scotland

Note: In some isolated cases, there may be restrictions on the import of seeds and plants. Readers outside Great Britain are well advised to check their local situation.

VEGETABLES

Sir John Sinclair, from Scotland's far north, who helped to compile the first Statistical Account of his country, had this to say: 'Onions used to form the favourite bon-bons of the Highlander, who with a few of these and an oatcake, would travel an incredible distance, and live for days without other food.' While the Scottish climate limits the number of different vegetables that can be grown, their quality has always been undeniable.

Tradition has it that the potato was brought from Virginia to Britain by Sir Walter Raleigh in Elizabethan times. Scotland, however, has made the humble tattie her own. Not only do the Scots cultivate excellent varieties — like Pentland Dell, Arran Pilot and Arran Banner — but they have the cooks to match them. The secret, like most culinary ones, is simple. After the potatoes have been well boiled in salted water, and strained, they should be thoroughly dried. This is best done by leaving them in the pot after draining off the water, replacing them on the hot stove for a moment or two, and shaking them very well until all the remaining water has been steamed off. If you want 'chappet' — mashed — tatties, add a seasoning of pepper and extra salt to taste. Beat in butter or milk — butter is preferable as milk can make the end product leathery.

If the potatoes are to be served in their jackets, scrub them well, leave whole, and before boiling cut off the skin around the centre to a width of about 2 cm (¾ in) depending on the size of the potato. (Fry any remainder for breakfast, or make tattie scones from the recipe on p. 92.) This is a different method of cooking jacket potatoes to the one practised in Ireland, where they are cooked in their skins after a minimum, if any, scrubbing, then peeled when cooked, before serving.

BEETROOT

Beetroot is a very successful garden root crop in Scotland. The following three beetroot recipes are old favourites and give variation.

Pickled Beetroot

Wash the beets carefully, avoid damaging the skin or they will bleed. Cook in boiling, salted water — 25 g (1 oz) of salt to 500 ml (1 pint) of water — until tender (1½–2 hours depending on size). Cool, skin and slice or dice. Pack into jars and cover with spiced vinegar (see below). Cover the jars and store in the dark. Much work can be saved by storing in large jars and using as required, rather than using a lot of small containers.

Spiced Vinegar

1 litre (2 pints) malt vinegar
6 g (¼ oz) blade mace
12 g (½ oz) whole allspice
6 g (¼ oz) cloves
6 g (¼ oz) cinnamon bark
6 peppercorns

Put the vinegar and spices in a pan, and bring to the boil. Pour into a bowl, cover and leave to cool for 2 hours. Strain and cover beetroot. If the spices are not available, use 50 g (2 oz) pickling spice or buy ready-made spiced vinegar.

Note: The quality of the spiced vinegar is improved if the spices are left to stand unheated in the vinegar for up to two months.

Beetroot with Carrot

400 g (1 lb) cooked beetroot, peeled
200 g (½ lb) uncooked carrots, peeled
Salt and pepper
2 tablespoons French dressing or 1 tablespoon lemon juice

To serve hot

25 g (1 oz) butter
2 tablespoons wine vinegar
1 tablespoon sugar

Coarsely grate the beetroot and carrots and mix together in a bowl. Season lightly and serve cold sprinkled with French dressing or lemon juice and chopped parsley. To serve hot, melt the butter in a pan and add the mixed beet and carrots. Heat through, gently, with wine vinegar and sugar. Serve quickly, sprinkled with parsley. Serves 4–6.

Forfar Bridies (p. 50), Sausage Rolls (p. 48), Bacon and Potato Croquettes (p. 43), Haggis Flan (p. 35) and Meat Loaf (p. 45).

Beetroot in Arrowroot

75 g (3 oz) sugar
12 g (½ oz) arrowroot
125 ml (¼ pint) water
600 g (1½ lb) cooked beetroot,
  peeled and diced
3 tablespoons vinegar (wine or
  cider)
1 teaspoon salt
Freshly ground black pepper

Blend the sugar and arrowroot with a little of the water in a pan, then add the rest of the water and bring slowly to the boil, stirring frequently. Add beetroot and heat through very gently for about 5 minutes. Stir in vinegar, salt and pepper to taste and reheat before serving hot as a vegetable or cold as a salad. Serves 4–5.

Note: A little peeled, cored and chopped apple can be added with the beetroot, if liked.

BASHED NEEPS

Neeps are 'bashed', tatties 'chappet'. See neep brose, p. 77.

600 g (1½ lb) neeps (swedes),
  peeled
50 g (2 oz) butter
Salt and pepper
Little ground ginger (optional)
Chopped parsley

Cut swede into small pieces and cook in lightly salted boiling water till tender for 30–40 minutes. Drain very well then mash thoroughly. Beat in the butter and add salt and pepper to taste. If liked, add a little ground ginger to enhance the flavour (it doesn't taste of ginger). Serve in a hot dish with the top forked up and sprinkled with chopped parsley. Serves 4–5.

Note: Meg Dods recommended ginger with the comment: 'Ginger corrects the flatulent properties of this esculent.'

CLAPSHOT

300 g (¾ lb) swede, peeled and
  diced
400 g (1 lb) potatoes, peeled and
  diced
Salt and pepper
40 g (2 oz) butter
1 small onion, peeled and finely
  chopped

Place swede in a pan with boiling, salted water, cover and simmer for 15 minutes then add the potatoes and continue to cook until tender. Drain thoroughly, then mash well. Beat in plenty of seasoning, the butter and chopped onion. Serve very hot.

Note: It is essential to use a larger quantity of potato than swede or the finished dish will be too sloppy.

Top: Breakfast: Porridge (p. 77) with Morning Rolls — Butteries — (p. 88) and Grapefruit Marmalade (p. 108).

Bottom: High tea: Black Pudding (p. 79), Oatcakes (p. 79), Scotch Mutton Pies (p. 49), Tied Tailies (p. 19), Kippers (p. 15), Smoked Trout (p. 27), Haggis (p. 35) and Bashed Neeps (p. 71).

71

GREEN KAIL

This is made from the curly kail which survives the worst winter weather in Scottish vegetable gardens (not to be confused with cattle kail), in the 'kail-yaird'.

This vegetable dish is not to everyone's choice, although it is a pure vegetable soup. The 'bree' is used in kail brose, see p. 77.

800 g (2 lb) curly kail
Oatmeal
Little cream
Salt and pepper

Remove the strong shanks from the greens. Put into a saucepan enough water to cover the greens and bring to the boil. Add the prepared greens when the water is boiling. Boil for 1 hour, leaving them uncovered. Take the curly kail out, squeeze them free of liquor and chop finely or squeeze them through a sieve. Sprinkle with oatmeal and put back into pot with stock. Add a little warmed cream, with pepper and salt to taste. Stir, boil for a few minutes and serve with thin oatcakes.

LEEKS

After removing the outside leaves, the tops and roots, wash the leeks well. It may be necessary to cut down the length to remove all the dirt. Allow 1–3 leeks per person depending on size and wastage.

To boil: Cook in boiling, salted water until tender (20–30 minutes, depending on size). Drain well and serve with a white or cheese sauce.

To braise: After tying each head of leek securely, fry in butter for a few minutes. Put in an ovenproof dish, add stock, pepper and salt and a knob of butter. Cover and cook at 180°C (350°F, Gas 4) for 1–1½ hours. Serve, after removing string, with the stock.

HIGHLAND POTATO CAKES

600 g (1½ lb) potatoes
1 onion, peeled
6 rashers streaky bacon
Salt and pepper
Good pinch of ground nutmeg
25 g (1 oz) melted butter
Fat or dripping

Peel potatoes and mince (grind) coarsely with the onion and bacon. Drain off any liquor. Add the seasonings, nutmeg and melted butter and mix well. Leave to stand for about 30 minutes, if possible, then fry tablespoons of the mixture in shallow fat for about 6–8 minutes each side till golden brown and cooked through. Press the cakes down during cooking with the back of a palette knife. Drain on absorbent paper and serve hot.

Note: The potatoes and onion can be finely grated and the bacon finely chopped, if preferred.

CHAPPET TATTIES AND MILK

This was a regular dish when money was scarce or potatoes and milk plentiful but, cost apart, it is a dish to be enjoyed by anyone. It is, however, apt to expand waistlines.

Boil good potatoes and dry them well. Add butter and pepper and extra salt to taste and mash. Serve with a bowl of milk.

POTATO OMELETTE

100 g (4 oz) boiled potatoes
3 eggs, separated
3 tablespoons milk
½ teaspoon lemon juice
Pinch of ground nutmeg or mace
Salt and pepper
1 tablespoon freshly chopped
  parsley (optional)
25 g (1 oz) butter

Press the potato through a sieve or mash very smoothly, then beat in the egg yolks, milk, lemon juice, nutmeg or mace, salt, pepper, and parsley if used. Whisk egg whites till very stiff then fold into the mixture. Melt butter in a frying pan and when hot pour in the egg mixture. Cook gently till browned underneath then place under a moderate grill and cook until omelette is set and golden brown. Carefully slide onto a hot dish and serve. Serves 1–2.

Note: 50 g (2 oz) grated cheese can be added to the mixture or sprinkled onto the omelette before grilling.

STOVIES

These are easy to cook, and a great favourite on a cold winter night, especially with children. Roast beef dripping, if available, gives the best result.

40 g (2 oz) butter or dripping
1–2 large onions, peeled and thinly sliced
400–800 g (1–2 lb) potatoes, peeled and thickly sliced
125–150 ml ($\frac{1}{4}$–$\frac{1}{2}$ pint) water
Salt and black pepper

Melt butter or dripping in a heavy pan and add onions. Fry gently without colouring, then add the potatoes, water, and plenty of seasoning. Bring to the boil, cover tightly and simmer very gently for 45–60 minutes till soft. Stir occasionally to prevent sticking during cooking. Alternatively, the stovies can be put into a heavy casserole, tightly covered and cooked at 150°C (300°C, Gas 2) for about 2 hours or till soft and mushy. Serves 3–6.

EGGS

A Highland lady was heard to say recently that she was not at all happy about having to buy eggs from battery hens. She much preferred eggs from 'running about' hens.

Another delicacy to be enjoyed by all who can find or buy a supply is the egg of the blackheaded gull, hardboiled and served with celery salt. The egg of the herring gull is sometimes used, but it tends to have a strong fishy taste and is not recommended. There are no restrictions on gathering blackheaded gulls' eggs, but do take them as soon after laying as possible, and seek local advice before embarking on a gathering expedition. The eggs of the plover, whaup, peewit, teuchat or lapwing (many names for just one species) were, until the bird was protected, an even greater delicacy, but to take them from the nest is now illegal.

BAKED EGGS

100 g (4 oz) potted shrimps or peeled prawns
4–8 eggs
Salt and pepper
6–8 tablespoons double (heavy) cream
Parsley sprigs

Heat shrimps gently in a pan then divide between 4 individual heatproof dishes (or one larger dish). If using prawns place in well buttered dishes. Carefully break eggs over the shellfish and season with salt and pepper. Spoon cream over the eggs and cook at 190°C (375°F, Gas 5) for 15–25 minutes till eggs are just set. Serve immediately with fingers of hot toast or oatcakes, garnished with parsley.

Note: For a change replace shrimps with chopped bacon or ham, or fried onion, or fried chopped tomatoes or mushrooms.

SCOTCH EGGS

4 hardboiled eggs
200 g (½ lb) sausagemeat or
   skinned sausages
1 egg, beaten
Breadcrumbs or raspings
Deep fat for frying
Parsley sprigs

Shell the eggs. Divide the sausagemeat into 4, and flatten each piece. Wrap a piece round each egg, keeping it as even as possible, moulding to the egg and making sure there are no cracks. Brush with beaten egg and roll in breadcrumbs till well coated. Fry in moderately hot, deep fat for 6–8 minutes till golden brown and the sausagemeat is cooked through. Drain well. Serve hot, garnished with parsley, with a tomato or mushroom sauce, or cold, cut in half, with salads.

RICH EGG SAUCE

50 g (2 oz) butter or margarine
50 g (2 oz) flour
375 ml (¾ pint) milk
Salt and pepper
1 teaspoon Worcestershire sauce
Good squeeze of lemon juice
2–3 hardboiled eggs, chopped
2 tablespoons freshly chopped
   parsley (optional)
125 ml (¼ pint) single (light)
   cream or milk

Melt butter or margarine in a pan, stir in the flour and cook for 1–2 minutes. Gradually add the milk, stirring frequently, and bring slowly to the boil. Add seasonings to taste, Worcestershire sauce, lemon juice, eggs, and parsley if used. Simmer gently for 3 minutes then stir in the cream and reheat gently. Serve with fish, vegetables, potatoes, etc. Serves 4–6.

Note: To make a supper dish, cook about 500 g (1–1½ lb) vegetables (mixed or one variety) and place in a heatproof dish. Cover with egg sauce and 2 tablespoons breadcrumbs and cook at 220°C (425°F, Gas 7) for about 20–30 minutes till really hot and golden brown.

OATMEAL

Before he really sampled Scottish hospitality in 1773, Dr Johnson is said to have defined 'oats' as: 'Food for horses in England and men in Scotland'. A Scotsman (not, we think, the sycophantic Boswell) riposted, 'And where, sir, will you find such horses, *or* such men?'

The ground grain of oats or corn has always been used extensively in Scottish cooking. While a number of other recipes in this book call for the inclusion of oatmeal, the recipes in this section illustrate its use as the main ingredient of a dish.

The domination of oatmeal (and potatoes) in the Scottish rural diet can in part be accounted for by the old method of paying farm servants (labourers). Until the outbreak of the Second World War, a large amount of the wages was paid in kind. The following example applied on a large farm in Banffshire; with a weekly wage of £1.25 to £1.50, the worker received in addition:

1 ton of coal every six months
1 load of firewood every six months
1 ton of potatoes annually
3 pints (1.5 litres) of milk daily (skimmed milk was available as a free extra if the farm sold cream or made cheese)
1 boll (63.5 kg/140 lb) of oatmeal every six months

Plain brose was a breakfast dish; invariably the meal was placed in wooden bowls at night and heated gently on the hob till morning. Hot water was made ready and every man made his own brose before starting work—'yokin' time', as it was called. As a dinnertime extra there would sometimes be neep (swede) brose and kail brose (see recipe p. 77).

St Andrews University still has a holiday on 'Meal Monday' and, till quite recently, it was also a holiday in Edinburgh. This marked the weekend during the Michaelmas term when the farmers' undergraduate sons returned home to replenish their supply of meal to keep them going until the end of the year. This was an important part of the parents' contribution to the costs of educating a son, as meal was in many cases the main diet.

While oatmeal, in various grades, is plentiful in Scotland, it is not always easy to find elsewhere. When you do find a supply, buy a stock—it will keep well in an airtight container.

PORRIDGE

Approx 1 litre (1½–2 pints)
  water
Approx 150 g (6 oz) medium
  oatmeal
2 teaspoons salt

Bring the water to the boil in a saucepan then slowly add oatmeal, stirring with a porridge spurtle or the handle of a long wooden spoon to prevent the mixture becoming lumpy. Simmer gently for about 10 minutes then add the salt. When it is boiling steadily, turn down heat as low as possible and cook very gently for 20–30 minutes according to taste. Serve in wooden bowls or cold soup plates, with small individual bowls of single (light) cream or rich milk. Dip each spoonful of porridge into the cold milk before eating.

Note: Sprinkle with uncooked meal to cover and, if you like it, add a little sugar.

BROSE

It was not unusual for West Highland fishermen to carry oatmeal on the boat and dip a handful of it in the seawater and thus create a type of brose. The lowland traveller used spring water and apparently went without salt.

Medium oatmeal
Pinch of salt
Boiling water
Butter

Put the amount of oatmeal required into a basin with the salt. Pour enough boiling water over it to wet the meal thoroughly and stand it for a few minutes to let it swell, but do not let it cool. Beat in a good knob of butter and serve with cream or rich milk

Note: Neep (swede), turnip, kail (curly kail) and cabbage brose can be made as above using the boiling liquid from cooking the vegetables with a pinch of sugar; serve with the vegetable stock and cooked vegetables instead of milk or cream.

SKIRLIE

50 g (2 oz) shredded suet or
  dripping
2 large onions, peeled and sliced
100 g (4 oz) medium oatmeal
Salt and pepper

Melt the suet or dripping in a hot pan then add the onions and fry until golden brown. Add enough of the oatmeal to absorb all the fat, keeping the mixture fairly thick, and season well. Cook slowly for about 10 minutes, stirring frequently. Serve as an accompaniment to any meat or game dish or as the main dish surrounded by a border of creamed potatoes. Serves 3–4.

OATMEAL HODGILS

100 g (4 oz) coarse oatmeal
50 g (2 oz) dripping
Salt and pepper
Chopped chives, onions or shallots

Mix all the ingredients together and form into small balls. Drop into boiling broth or soup and cook for 20 minutes.

CRANACHAN (CREAM CROWDIE)

100 g (4 oz) medium oatmeal
160 ml ($\frac{1}{3}$ pint) double (heavy)
  cream
125 ml ($\frac{1}{4}$ pint) single (light)
  cream
Fine sugar to taste
Few drops vanilla essence or any
  liqueur or rum
Fresh raspberries, strawberries,
  etc

Toast the oatmeal until lightly browned either under a grill, in the oven or in a frying pan. Cool. Whip the creams together until thick but not too stiff and add sugar and essence to taste. Fold in oatmeal followed by the fresh fruit. Serve chilled in individual glasses immediately after making.

Note: If the coarse grade of oatmeal is used it toasts better and increases the nutty taste. Do not try to keep, otherwise the crowdie goes stodgy.

OATMEAL BISCUITS

150 g (6 oz) plain flour
Bare $\frac{1}{4}$ teaspoon bicarbonate of
  soda (baking soda)
Bare $\frac{1}{2}$ teaspoon cream of tartar
Good pinch of salt
100 g (4 oz) medium oatmeal
50 g (2 oz) fine sugar
75 g (3 oz) margarine or butter
Approx 3 tablespoons milk

Sieve flour, soda, cream of tartar and salt into a bowl and mix in oatmeal and sugar. Rub in margarine or butter then add sufficient milk to give a fairly soft dough. Carefully roll out thinly on an oatmeal covered surface, cut into 6 cm (2$\frac{1}{2}$ in) rounds and place on greased baking sheets. Prick well and cook at 180°C (350°F, Gas 4) for 25–30 minutes till lightly coloured. Cool on a wire rack. Makes 20–25 biscuits.

OATCAKES

In a country home, fresh oatcakes were baked on the girdle every day. They were dried off on a metal rack or toaster which was hung by hooks onto the front of the kitchen fire.

Oatcakes are known as 'bread' (breid) or bannocks.

100 g (4 oz) fine oatmeal
Pinch of salt
Good pinch of bicarbonate of
  soda (baking soda)
1 teaspoon bacon fat or dripping
Hot water

Place the oatmeal in a bowl with salt and soda. Melt the fat and add to the oatmeal with sufficient hot water to make a stiff paste. Knead the mixture into a smooth ball and roll out on an oatmeal covered surface as thinly as possible, keeping the edges neat. Cut into a round then into 4 or 8 pieces. Place on a moderately hot girdle and cook slowly until the edges begin to curl up and the underneath is dry. Toast the other side under a moderate grill or place in a warm oven to dry out. Store in an airtight container. (If a girdle is not available, use a strong frying pan.)

BLACK PUDDINGS

Black puddings can be bought ready-made; if you cannot buy them locally, then try this recipe—but only if your butcher can supply the necessary skins and pig's blood.

1 litre (2 pints) pig's blood
250 ml (½ pint) warmed skimmed
  milk
200 g (½ lb) medium oatmeal
200 g (½ lb) shredded suet
1 medium onion, finely chopped
1 tablespoon salt
1 tablespoon freshly ground
  black pepper
Commercial sausage skin or tripe
  skin

Put pig's blood into a large basin, stir in the warmed skimmed milk, add the oatmeal, suet, onion, salt and pepper and mix all the ingredients well. Make sure the pudding skins are clean and dry, then tie one end with thin string. The skins may be tied into a ring or tied in shorter, sausage-like lengths but when filling with the mixture make sure that each section is only half filled, then tie off. Put them into near boiling water, bring to the boil and simmer for 1 hour, pricking them with a needle to release the air. Hang them up in a dry, cool place. When needed, put them into hot water for 10 minutes then broil or slice and fry or grill them.

MEALIE PUDDINGS (MEALIE JIMMIES)

Scottish butchers sell excellent mealie puddings ready for heating up. There are two methods: after separating them if tied, either cook in a pan by placing in cold water, bringing to the boil and simmering for 10 minutes, or put in a heatproof dish and place in a hot oven, 160°C (325°F, Gas 3), for 25 minutes. Serve piping hot, alone or with boiled potatoes, or as an extra to almost any meat dish. There are no rules; eat them as you enjoy them.

If you cannot buy mealie puddings locally the following recipe can be used, but only if your butcher can supply the necessary skins.

800 g (2 lb) medium oatmeal
400 g (1 lb) shredded suet
2 medium onions, finely chopped
1 tablespoon salt
1 tablespoon freshly ground
    black pepper
Commercial sausage skin or tripe
    skin

Toast oatmeal in oven, then mix with suet, onions, salt and pepper. Make sure the pudding skins are clean and dry, then tie one end with thin string. Tying either one length or several smaller lengths, three-quarters fill each section of skin with the oatmeal mixture and tie off. Boil for 1 hour, pricking with a needle to release the air. Allow to cool. When required, heat thoroughly in hot water or heat in the oven.

Note: These puddings will keep for months if hung up and kept dry. They were often buried in oatmeal in the girnel or meal-chest.

FITLESS COCK or MEALIE DUMPLING

200 g (8 oz) medium oatmeal
200 g (8 oz) shredded suet
1 large onion or 6 shallots, peeled
    and chopped
Salt and black pepper

Toast the oatmeal lightly under the grill or in a moderate oven. Mix with the suet, onion or shallots, and plenty of salt and pepper. Do not add any liquid to bind together. Mould the mixture roughly into the shape of a chicken. Tie loosely in a clean floured cloth, leaving plenty of room for oatmeal to swell. Place on a plate in a large saucepan of boiling water and simmer, uncovered, for 1½ hours, topping up with more boiling water as necessary to keep the dumpling covered. Remove carefully and unwrap. The dumpling is usually served with boiled fowl but can also be served by itself with mashed potatoes.

Note: A beaten egg is sometimes added to the mixture but this is not at all necessary. The suet melts as it cooks and binds the dumpling together.

BAKING

The Scottish housewife is an enthusiastic home baker of bread, cakes, biscuits, baps and scones. The deep freeze has added new interest to the art, and it is now possible to keep quantities of good quality home baking fresh for future use— though probably not in such amounts as that required by a single Meg Dods recipe: her 'Scotch half-peck bun' contained among many other things half a peck (a gallon or 4 litres) of flour and 6 lb (3 kg) of mixed fruit.

There are some items which, in spite of the high quality of home baking, are baked even better by the bakery. In the north-east of Scotland, roughly from Aberdeen to Inverness, the 'buttery rowies' or morning rolls are still delivered to the door by the baker in the early morning, and are eagerly awaited. Try the recipe on p. 88.

Many a north-east Scotsman, returning from the south or abroad, always felt he was home when, coming off an early morning train at Aberdeen, he had breakfast in the station buffet or (if business was prosperous) at the Station Hotel, where probably the best breakfast in the world is served: thinly sliced Ayrshire cured bacon, fresh free-range eggs, poached Aberdeen smoked haddock, morning rolls, local butter, marmalade, and possibly heather honey.

The main meal of the day in Scotland is midday dinner, the evening meal being high tea—if something cooked was served then it was called 'kitchie'. This was when the home baking came into its own: scones, shortbread and cake, with jams, jellies and honey, if bees were kept.

DUNDEE CAKE

250 g (10 oz) plain flour
Pinch of salt
½ teaspoon baking powder
50 g (2 oz) blanched almonds
100 g (4 oz) currants
100 g (4 oz) raisins
100 g (4 oz) sultanas (white raisins)
100 g (4 oz) chopped mixed peel
Grated rind of 1 orange and 1 lemon
200 g (8 oz) butter
200 g (8 oz) light soft brown sugar (or fine sugar)
4 large eggs
A little milk

Grease and line a 20 cm (8 in) round cake tin. Sieve flour with salt and baking powder. Chop half the almonds and mix with currants, raisins, sultanas, peel and grated rinds. Cream butter and sugar till light and fluffy, then beat in eggs one at a time following each with 1 tablespoon of the flour. Fold in remaining flour followed by the mixed fruit. Add a little milk if necessary to give a dropping consistency. Turn into the tin, making a slight hollow in the centre of the cake. Split the remaining almonds and arrange over the surface. Bake at 160°C (325°F, Gas 3) for 2½–3 hours, covering with greaseproof paper if the top is getting too brown. Cool the cake in the tin for 20 minutes before turning out onto a wire rack to get cold.

SKYE CAKE

300 g (12 oz) plain flour
¾ teaspoon bicarbonate of soda
  (baking soda)
¾ teaspoon ground cinnamon
¾ teaspoon ground nutmeg
150 g (6 oz) butter, cut into small
  pieces
150 g (6 oz) demerara sugar
100 g (4 oz) chopped mixed peel
300 g (12 oz) currants
3 eggs
125 ml (¼ pint) stout or brown
  ale

Grease and line a 20 cm (8 in) round cake tin. Sieve flour, soda, cinnamon and nutmeg into a bowl. Add butter and rub in till mixture resembles fine breadcrumbs. Add sugar, peel and currants and mix well. Beat the eggs and add gradually with the stout. Turn into the tin and bake at 160°C (325°F, Gas 3) for 2–2¼ hours. Cool the cake in the tin for 30 minutes before turning out onto a wire rack to get cold. This cake is improved if wrapped in greaseproof paper and foil and kept for a week before eating.

SCOTS SEED CAKE

175 g (7 oz) plain flour
1 teaspoon baking powder
½ teaspoon ground cinnamon
¼ teaspoon ground nutmeg
100 g (4 oz) butter
100 g (4 oz) fine sugar
3 eggs
75 g (3 oz) chopped mixed peel
50 g (2 oz) blanched almonds,
  chopped (optional)
2 teaspoons caraway seeds
A little milk

Grease and line a 16 cm (6–7 in) round cake tin. Sieve together flour, baking powder, cinnamon and nutmeg. Cream butter and sugar till pale, light and fluffy. Beat in the eggs one at a time, following each with 1 teaspoon of the flour. Fold in remaining flour. Add peel, almonds if used and caraway seeds. The mixture should easily drop from a spoon—add a little milk if necessary to obtain the correct consistency. Turn into the tin and bake at 160°C (325°F, Gas 3) for 1¼–1½ hours. Cool the cake in the tin for 10 minutes before turning out onto a wire rack to get cold.

DIET CAKE

200 g (8 oz) fine sugar
100 g (4 oz) butter
3 large eggs, beaten
Grated rind of ½ lemon
¼ teaspoon ground cinnamon
150 g (6 oz) plain flour
Icing (confectioner's) sugar or
  glacé icing (see p. 98)

Grease and line a 20 cm (8 in) round cake tin. Cream sugar and butter till light and fluffy. Add eggs and beat for 10–15 minutes. Add lemon rind and cinnamon then gradually add the sieved flour, beating well after each addition. Turn the mixture into the tin and bake at 190°C (375°F, Gas 5) for about 45 minutes till well risen and lightly browned. Five minutes before it is ready dust the top of the cake with icing sugar and return to the oven. Cool for a few minutes in the tin before turning out onto a wire rack. If preferred, the icing sugar topping can be omitted and the cake iced when cold.

RASPBERRY SPONGE

3 eggs
75 g (3 oz) fine sugar
40 g (1½ oz) plain flour
40 g (1½ oz) self-raising flour
Pinch of salt
Approx 140 g (4–6 oz) raspberries
A little sugar
125 ml (¼ pint) double (heavy)
  cream

Grease and line a 20 cm (8 inch) deep sandwich tin. Whisk eggs and sugar in a bowl over a pan of hot water till thick and fluffy. Remove from the heat and whisk for a few minutes more. Sieve flours and salt and fold gradually into the egg mixture. Turn into the prepared tin and cook at 220°F (425°C, Gas 7) for about 15 minutes till firm. Turn onto a wire rack and cool. Mash raspberries with sugar to taste and whip cream stiffly. Split cake in half and fill with one layer of crushed raspberries and one of cream. Replace lid and sprinkle top with fine or icing (confectioner's) sugar.

Note: Thawed and drained frozen raspberries can be used in place of fresh ones, or try a thick layer of raspberry jam.

WHISKY CAKE

200 g (8 oz) seedless raisins
125 ml (¼ pint) water
100 g (4 oz) butter
125 g (5 oz) soft brown sugar
1 large egg
150 g (6 oz) plain flour
1 teaspoon bicarbonate of soda
  (baking soda)
½ teaspoon ground nutmeg
½ teaspoon ground cloves
100 g (4 oz) walnuts or blanched
  almonds, chopped
2 tablespoons whisky

Put raisins and water in a pan, bring to the boil, cover and simmer gently for 15 minutes. Drain and make liquor up to 125 ml (¼ pint) with more water. Cream the butter and sugar till light and fluffy then beat in the egg. Sieve flour with soda and spices and add to the creamed mixture with the raisin liquor. Add raisins, nuts and whisky and beat well. Divide between two greased and lined 20 cm (8 in) straight-sided sandwich tins. Bake at 180°C (350°F, Gas 4) for 30–35 minutes. Turn out carefully onto a wire rack and cool.

Icing

75 g (3 oz) butter
1 egg yolk
200 g (8 oz) icing (confectioner's)
  sugar
1 tablespoon whisky
Walnut halves or toasted almonds
  for decoration

To make the icing, melt the butter in a pan then beat in the egg yolk followed by the icing sugar, a little at a time. Finally add whisky and use three-quarters of the icing to sandwich cakes together. Decorate top with whirls of remaining icing and walnut halves or toasted almonds.

BLACK BUN

Black bun baked well in advance is served on Hogmanay and New Year's Day to the 'first footer' who calls to wish the household a Happy New Year. It is of course served with a dram.

Pastry

200 g (8 oz) plain flour
Pinch of salt
100 g (4 oz) butter
Water
Beaten egg for glaze

For the pastry, sieve the flour and salt into a bowl and rub in butter till the mixture resembles fine breadcrumbs. Add sufficient water to mix to a smooth firm dough. Roll out two-thirds of the pastry to a round about 35 cm (14 in) in diameter and use it to carefully line a greased 20 cm (8 in) round cake tin. Take care not to pleat or split the pastry, and rest edges over the top of the tin.

Filling

400 g (1 lb) currants
400 g (1 lb) raisins
50 g (2 oz) chopped mixed peel
100 g (4 oz) blanched almonds, chopped
100 g (4 oz) brown sugar
200 g (8 oz) plain flour
1 teaspoon each cinnamon, ground ginger, ground allspice, cream of tartar and bicarbonate of soda (baking soda)
1 egg, beaten
8 tablespoons whisky
Approx 4 tablespoons milk

For the filling, mix together the dried fruit, peel, almonds and sugar. Sieve the flour with the spices, cream of tartar and soda, and add to the fruit. Add egg, whisky and sufficient milk to just moisten the mixture. Carefully pack into the pastry case and fold the pastry edges over. Roll the remaining pastry into a 20 cm (8 in) lid. Brush the edges with beaten egg and position the lid. Press well down and lightly crimp the edge. Make 6 or 8 holes right through the cake with a skewer and prick the whole top of the pastry with a fork. Brush with beaten egg and bake at 180°C (350°F, Gas 4) for 2½–3 hours, covering the top with foil if it becomes too brown. Cool in the tin for at least 30 minutes before turning out onto a wire rack to get cold.

Note: This cake is better made several weeks in advance, for it matures and mellows with keeping—some people keep it for up to a year before eating.

PARLIES (PARLIAMENT CAKES)

The Scottish Parliament (or the Three Estates) used to meet in a building behind St Giles on Edinburgh's Royal Mile. Round about 1700 they used to enjoy marmalade on their 'meridian bannock', taken with a 'houp o' sma' yill'—light ale—about twelve o'clock.

200 g (8 oz) plain flour
2 teaspoons ground ginger
100 g (4 oz) soft brown sugar
100 g (4 oz) butter or margarine
100 g (4 oz) black treacle

Sieve flour and ginger into a bowl and mix with the sugar. Melt the butter in a pan, add treacle and bring to the boil. Pour into the dry ingredients and mix quickly with a wooden spoon. When smooth and cool enough to handle, roll out on lightly greased baking trays to 3–6 mm ($\frac{1}{8}$–$\frac{1}{4}$ in) thickness. Cut into 8 cm (3 in) squares and prick the dough all over. Bake at 150°C (300°F, Gas 2) for 25–30 minutes till dark brown but still soft. Separate and cool on trays for 3–5 minutes till firm enough to move to a wire rack—they crisp up as they cool. Makes approx 20.

CRULLAS

300 g (12 oz) plain flour
$\frac{1}{2}$ teaspoon bicarbonate of soda (baking soda)
$\frac{1}{4}$ teaspoon cream of tartar
$\frac{1}{4}$ teaspoon salt
$\frac{1}{4}$ teaspoon ground ginger or nutmeg
50 g (2 oz) butter
50 g (2 oz) fine sugar
2 eggs, beaten
Approx 2 tablespoons buttermilk or sour milk (see note below)
Deep fat or oil for frying
Icing (confectioner's) sugar

Sieve together flour, soda, cream of tartar, salt and spice. Cream butter and sugar till light and fluffy then beat in eggs followed by dry ingredients and sufficient buttermilk or sour milk to give a firm dough. Turn onto a floured surface and roll out thinly. Cut into rectangles 20×8 cm (8×3 in), then divide each piece into three 2.5 cm (1 in) wide strips leaving the ends uncut. Plait the strips then dampen ends and stick together firmly to keep plait together. Fry in hot oil for a few minutes each side until golden brown. Drain on absorbent paper and sprinkle with icing sugar whilst still hot. Serve warm or cold. Makes approx 12.

Note: To make sour milk, add 1 teaspoon of lemon juice to each 125 ml ($\frac{1}{4}$ pint) milk.

SODA BREAD

400 g (1 lb) plain flour
1 teaspoon salt
1½ teaspoons bicarbonate of soda
(baking soda)
1 teaspoon cream of tartar
25 g (1 oz) lard or margarine
Approx 250 ml (½ pint) buttermilk or sour milk (see previous
recipe)

Sieve flour, salt, soda and cream of tartar into a bowl
and rub in the fat till mixture resembles fine breadcrumbs. Add sufficient buttermilk or sour milk to
give a soft elastic dough. Turn onto a floured surface
and shape quickly into one or two round cakes. Place
on a floured baking sheet, dredge with more flour and
score into sections. Cook at 220°C (425°F, Gas 7) for
about 30 minutes till well risen, lightly brown, and
firm underneath. Cool on a wire rack wrapped in a
clean tea towel.

Note: To make brown soda bread use 200 g (8 oz)
each of plain flour and wholemeal flour.

SPONGY GINGERBREAD

400 g (1 lb) plain flour
2 teaspoons ground ginger
50 g (2 oz) margarine
50 g (2 oz) lard (shortening)
200 g (8 oz) fine sugar
200 g (8 oz) golden syrup
1 egg, beaten
250 ml (½ pint) milk
2 teaspoons bicarbonate of soda
(baking soda)
2 teaspoons vinegar

Grease and line a 23 cm (9 in) square cake tin or a flat
tin, 25×20×5 cm (10×8×2 in). Sieve flour and ginger
together. Place fats, sugar and syrup in a pan and heat
till the fat has melted. Add dry ingredients with the
egg, milk and soda blended with vinegar. Beat till
smooth then pour into the tin and bake at 160°C
(325°F, Gas 3) for about 1¼ hours till well risen and
firm to the touch. Cool in the tin for 10 minutes before
turning out onto a wire rack to cool. Serve plain or
covered with glacé icing (see p. 98) and small pieces of
stem or crystallized ginger.

GINGERBREAD LOAF

200 g (8 oz) plain flour
1 teaspoon mixed spice
½ teaspoon bicarbonate of soda
(baking soda)
1½ tablespoons ground ginger
50 g (2 oz) chopped mixed peel
(optional)
75 g (3 oz) soft brown sugar
100 g (4 oz) margarine
200 g (8 oz) black treacle (or half
treacle and half golden syrup)
250 ml (½ pint) milk
1 egg, beaten

Grease and line a 22.5 × 12.5 cm (9 × 5 in) loaf tin.
Sieve flour, spice, soda and ginger into a bowl and mix
in peel and sugar. Melt margarine and treacle in a pan
then add the milk and mix well. Add the beaten egg
to the dry ingredients with the treacle liquid and beat
till smooth. The mixture should resemble a thick
brown sauce. Pour into the tin and cook at 180°C
(350°F, Gas 4) for 1¼–1½ hours till firm. Cool in the
tin for 20 minutes before turning out onto a wire rack
to cool. Wrap in foil for 2 to 7 days before use.

Baking day: Scotch Crumpets (p. 92), Glasgow Floury Baps (p. 89),
Soda Bread (p. 86), Oatcakes (p. 79), Dundee Cake (p. 81),
Raspberry Sponge (p. 83), Scotch Shortbread (p. 93), Rich Floury
Scones (p. 89) and Gingerbread Loaf (p. 86).

CURRANT LOAF

400 g (1 lb) strong plain flour
2 teaspoons salt
25 g (1 oz) lard (shortening)
150–200 g (6–8 oz) currants
50 g (2 oz) chopped mixed peel (optional)
12 g ($\frac{1}{2}$ oz) fresh yeast
1 teaspoon fine sugar
250 ml ($\frac{1}{2}$ pint) warm milk
Little sugar syrup

Grease two 400 g (1 lb) loaf tins. Sieve flour and salt into a bowl. Add lard and rub in. Mix in currants and peel. Cream yeast with the sugar in a basin then gradually add the milk; add to dry ingredients, mixing to a soft dough. Knead for about 10 minutes on a lightly floured surface till dough is smooth and no longer sticky. Place in an oiled polythene bag, tie loosely and put in a warm place for about an hour till doubled in size. Knead to remove air bubbles and make a firm dough. Divide in half and shape to fit the tins. Place in tins to come just over half full and press corners down. Return to the polythene bag and put in a warm place for dough to rise to the top of the tins — about 30 minutes. Bake at 230°C (450°F, Gas 8) for 15 minutes then reduce to 190°C (375°F, Gas 5) for a further 25–35 minutes. When ready the loaf will sound hollow if the base is tapped. While still hot, brush with sugar syrup made from boiling 2 tablespoons of sugar in 2 tablespoons of water for 1–2 minutes, then leave to cool on a wire rack.

SELKIRK BANNOCK

400 g (1 lb) strong plain flour
1 teaspoon salt
1 teaspoon fine sugar
Good 250 ml ($\frac{1}{2}$ pint) warm milk and water mixed
3 teaspoons dried yeast
50 g (2 oz) softened lard (shortening)
100 g (4 oz) fine sugar
150–200 g (6–8 oz) sultanas (white raisins) or raisins
50 g (2 oz) chopped mixed peel
50 g (2 oz) softened butter

Grease a deep 20×25 cm (8×10 in) tin. Sieve flour and salt into a bowl. Dissolve sugar in the milk and water, sprinkle on dried yeast and leave in a warm place for 10 minutes till frothy. Add to dry ingredients with more water if necessary to make a soft dough. Knead lightly for about 5 minutes then put in an oiled polythene bag in a warm place until doubled in size. Knead to knock out the air bubbles then roll out thinly to an oblong. Evenly cover two-thirds of the dough with small pieces of the lard and sprinkle with half of the sugar, sultanas, and peel. Fold the bottom third of dough upwards and the top third down to make an envelope shape as for flaky pastry. Give dough a half turn and repeat with the butter and remaining fruit and sugar. Roll and fold once more then shape to fit the tin, pressing the corners of the dough well into the tin. Cover with oiled polythene and leave to rise in a warm place for about 40 minutes till doubled in size. Cook at 200°C (400°F, Gas 6) for 45–60

Clootie Dumpling (p. 99), Eve's Pudding (p. 99), Grosset Mould (p. 103) and Shivering Tam (p. 101).

minutes till well browned and firm to the touch. Turn out and cool on a wire rack. Serve sliced either buttered or plain.

Note: If using fresh yeast cream 20 g ($\frac{3}{4}$ oz) with the sugar till liquid then add to the warm milk and water and proceed.

MORNING ROLLS
(BUTTERIES OR ROWIES)

The butteries or rowies are quite distinct from the floury breakfast baps so popular in Glasgow and the South of Scotland generally. (See the recipe on the opposite page.)

400 g (1 lb) strong plain flour
$\frac{1}{2}$ teaspoon salt
25 g (1 oz) fresh yeast
1 tablespoon sugar
250 ml ($\frac{1}{2}$ pint) plus approx 3 tablespoons warm water
150 g (6 oz) softened butter

Sieve flour and salt into a bowl. Cream yeast with the sugar till liquid then add to dry ingredients with sufficient water to mix to a fairly soft dough. Knead lightly on a floured surface for 5–10 minutes then place in a lightly oiled polythene bag for about 30–60 minutes till doubled in size. Turn onto a floured surface and knead to knock out the air bubbles and give a smooth dough. Roll out to a rectangle about 20×45 cm (8×18 in). Divide butter into three and dot one portion all over the top two-thirds of the dough. Fold bottom third upward and top third down like an envelope as for making flaky pastry. Press lightly, put into the oiled polythene bag and place in the refrigerator for 10–15 minutes. Repeat twice with remaining butter, giving dough a half turn for each rolling. Then roll out carefully to about 1 cm ($\frac{1}{2}$–$\frac{3}{4}$ in) thickness and cut into ovals or rounds approx 6–8 cm ($2\frac{1}{2}$–3 in). Place on floured baking sheets, cover lightly with oiled polythene and put in a warm place to rise for about 40 minutes till doubled in size. Bake at 200°C (400°F, Gas 6) for about 20 minutes. Cool on a wire rack and eat while still warm. Makes approx 15.

Note: If using dried yeast, dissolve sugar in the warm liquid, sprinkle 1 tablespoon dried yeast over it and leave in a warm place for about 10 minutes till frothy.

FLOURY BAPS

400 g (1 lb) strong plain flour
1 teaspoon salt
50 g (2 oz) lard
12 g ($\frac{1}{2}$ oz) fresh yeast
1 teaspoon sugar
250 ml ($\frac{1}{2}$ pint) warm milk and
    water mixed

Flour two baking sheets. Sieve flour and salt into a bowl. Rub in the lard. Cream yeast and sugar till liquid then slowly add the milk and water. Add to the dry ingredients and mix to a firm dough (adding a little more flour if necessary) till it leaves the side of the bowl clean. Turn onto a lightly floured surface and knead for 5–10 minutes till smooth. Place in an oiled polythene bag, loosely tied, and put to rise in a warm place for about an hour till doubled in size. Knead dough lightly to knock out the bubbles then divide into 10–12 even-sized pieces. Knead each piece into a ball then roll on a floured surface to an oval about 1 cm ($\frac{1}{2}$ in) thick. Place well apart on the baking sheets and loosely cover with oiled polythene. Return to a warm place to rise until doubled in size — about 20–30 minutes. Press each bap gently in the centre with three fingers to prevent blistering. Dredge with flour and cook at 220°C (425°F, Gas 7) for 15–20 minutes till well risen, lightly browned and hollow sounding when the base is tapped. Cool on a wire rack. Makes 10–12 rolls.

Note: If using dried yeast dissolve the sugar in the milk and water and sprinkle on 2 teaspoons of yeast. Leave in a warm place for about 10 minutes till frothy.

RICH FLOURY SCONES

200 g (8 oz) self-raising flour
Pinch of salt
50 g (2 oz) butter or margarine,
    cut into small pieces
25 g (1 oz) fine sugar
1 egg, beaten
85 ml (approx 3 fl. oz) milk to
    mix

Sieve flour and salt into a bowl, add the butter or margarine and rub in till mixture resembles fine breadcrumbs. Mix in sugar, then add egg and sufficient milk to give a soft dough. Knead lightly on a floured surface and level to a 2 cm ($\frac{3}{4}$ in) thickness. Either cut into triangles or 3–5 cm ($1\frac{1}{2}$–2 in) rounds and place on a floured baking sheet with the scones just touching each other. Dredge with flour and cook at 230°C (450°F, Gas 8) for about 10–15 minutes. Cool on a wire rack wrapped in a clean tea towel. Makes 8–10.

DATE TEA SCONE

200 g (8 oz) plain flour
½ teaspoon bicarbonate of soda
(baking soda)
1 teaspoon cream of tartar
Pinch of salt
25 g (1 oz) butter or margarine,
cut into small pieces
50 g (2 oz) stoned dates, chopped
2 teaspoons golden syrup
1 egg, beaten
Approx 4–6 tablespoons milk

Grease and flour a 19 cm (7–8 in) sandwich tin. Sieve the flour, soda, cream of tartar and salt into a bowl. Add the butter or margarine and rub in till the mixture resembles fine breadcrumbs. Add the dates. Melt syrup till runny then add with half the beaten egg and sufficient milk to give a fairly soft dough. Turn into the prepared tin and flatten lightly to fit. Mark into sections, brush with remaining egg and cook at 220°C (425°F, Gas 7) for about 20 minutes till firm to the touch and browned. Cool wrapped in a clean tea towel on a wire rack.

Note: To make a sweeter scone add 1 tablespoon of fine sugar with the dry ingredients.

GIRDLE SCONES

200 g (8 oz) plain flour
1 teaspoon bicarbonate of soda
(baking soda)
2 teaspoons cream of tartar
½ teaspoon salt
2 teaspoons sugar
25 g (1 oz) lard (shortening)
or margarine
125 ml (approx ¼ pint) sour milk
(see note p. 85)

Sieve flour, soda, cream of tartar and salt into a bowl, add sugar and rub in the fat. Mix to a soft but manageable dough with the milk. Divide dough in half and roll into 2 flat rounds about 5–10 mm (¼–½ in) thick. Heat a girdle or large heavy frying pan and dust with flour. Cut each scone round into 6 triangles and cook on the girdle for about 5 minutes till evenly brown on one side. Turn over and continue for a further 5 minutes till browned. Cool on a wire rack and serve warm with plenty of butter. Makes 12.

OVEN SCONES

200 g (8 oz) plain flour
¼ teaspoon salt
½ teaspoon bicarbonate of soda
(baking soda)
½ teaspoon cream of tartar
2 teaspoons fine sugar (optional)
50 g (2 oz) butter or margarine,
cut into small pieces
Approx 125 ml (¼ pint) milk to mix
1 egg, beaten (optional)

Sieve flour, salt, soda and cream of tartar into a bowl, add sugar if required and then the fat. Rub in fat till the mixture resembles fine breadcrumbs then add sufficient milk to mix to a soft elastic dough. Knead very lightly on a floured surface then roll or level dough to 2 cm (¾ in) thickness. Cut into 5 cm (2 in) rounds or triangles and place on a floured baking sheet. Brush with beaten egg or milk if liked, and cook at 230°C (450°F, Gas 8) for 10–15 minutes. Cool on a wire rack. Makes approx 10.

Note: Sour milk (see note p. 85) in place of fresh milk gives a very good flavour.

RICH DROP SCONES

100 g (4 oz) plain flour
½ teaspoon bicarbonate of soda
   (baking soda)
1 teaspoon cream of tartar
Good pinch of salt
1 teaspoon golden syrup
1 teaspoon fine sugar
1 egg
125 ml (¼ pint) milk

Sieve flour, soda, cream of tartar and salt into a bowl. Add syrup, sugar and egg and gradually beat in the milk to give a thick batter. Heat girdle or large heavy frying pan and wipe over with lard or oil. Cook tablespoons of the mixture placed well apart on the girdle until bubbles rise and begin to burst, then turn and continue for about 2 minutes till golden brown. Cool in a clean tea towel on a wire rack and eat while still warm, thickly buttered. Makes approx 10.

Note: These should be eaten the day they are made or they become rubbery.

WHOLEMEAL SCONES

75 g (3 oz) plain flour
1 teaspoon baking powder
Good pinch of salt
75 g (3 oz) wholemeal flour
40 g (1½ oz) butter or margarine,
   cut into small pieces
Approx 6–8 tablespoons milk,
   preferably sour (see note p. 85)

Sieve plain flour, baking powder and salt into a bowl and mix in wholemeal flour. Add fat and rub in till the mixture resembles fine breadcrumbs. Add sufficient milk to mix to a soft dough. Roll out lightly to about 1–2 cm (½–¾ in) thickness and cut into 5 cm (2 in) rounds. Place on a floured baking sheet and cook at 220°C (425°F, Gas 7) for 10–15 minutes. Cool on a wire rack wrapped in a clean tea towel. Makes 8–10.

TREACLE SCONES

200 g (8 oz) plain flour
½ teaspoon bicarbonate of soda
   (baking soda)
Bare ½ teaspoon cream of tartar
¼ teaspoon salt
½ teaspoon ground cinnamon
½ teaspoon ground ginger
   (optional)
2 teaspoons fine sugar
40 g (1½ oz) butter or margarine,
   cut into small pieces
1 tablespoon black treacle or
   golden syrup
Approx 6 tablespoons buttermilk
   or sour milk (see note p. 85)

Sieve flour, soda, cream of tartar, salt, cinnamon and ginger into a bowl and mix in sugar. Add butter or margarine to dry ingredients and rub in till the mixture resembles fine breadcrumbs. Melt treacle in 2 tablespoons buttermilk or sour milk in a pan then add to the flour mixture with sufficient buttermilk to give a fairly stiff dough. Knead lightly and form into a flat round 2 cm (¾ in) thick. Place on a lightly greased baking sheet and cut into eight triangles. Cook at 200°C (400°F, Gas 6) for about 15 minutes till well risen, and firm to the touch. Cool on a wire rack loosely wrapped in a clean tea towel.

TATTIE SCONES

200 g (½ lb) hot boiled potatoes
50 g (2 oz) butter, margarine or
   melted bacon fat
Salt to taste
Approx 75 g (2½ oz) plain flour

Mash the potatoes well then beat in the fat and salt to taste. Add as much flour as the mixture will take without becoming too dry. Turn onto a floured board and roll out to 5 mm (¼ in) thickness. Cut into 5 cm (2 in) rounds or larger rounds divided into 4, 6 or 8. Prick all over with a fork then cook on a fairly hot, lightly floured girdle till browned underneath, then turn and cook the other side — about 5 minutes altogether. Cool wrapped in a clean tea towel. Serve warm and buttered.

Note: These are best eaten on the same day they are made; otherwise store in an airtight container. For breakfast they fry very well with bacon and egg. Any leftover boiled or mashed potatoes may be used but, for best results, use while still hot. They can also be made from reconstituted dehydrated potatoes.

SCOTCH CRUMPETS

100 g (4 oz) self-raising flour
Pinch of salt
25 g (1 oz) sugar
1 egg, beaten
125 ml (¼ pint) milk
Lard (shortening) or oil

Place sieved flour and salt in a bowl with the sugar, then add the egg and milk and beat till bubbles rise to the surface. Heat a girdle or large heavy frying pan and rub lightly with lard or oil. Put tablespoons of the mixture onto the hot girdle well apart, and cook till bubbles rise to the surface. Turn carefully with a palette knife and cook for a further minute till golden brown. Place on a wire rack in a clean tea towel while the rest are cooked. Serve warm with plenty of butter and home-made jam or jelly. Makes approx 16.

Note: Like Tattie Scones, these should be eaten the day they are made, otherwise stored in an airtight container. They also fry very well with bacon and egg for breakfast.

BROONIE

150 g (6 oz) plain flour
1 teaspoon baking powder
Pinch of salt
2 teaspoons ground ginger
150 g (6 oz) medium oatmeal
50 g (2 oz) butter, cut into small
    pieces
100 g (4 oz) soft brown sugar
2 tablespoons black treacle
1 egg, beaten
Approx 250 ml ($\frac{1}{2}$ pint) butter-
    milk or sour milk (see note
    p. 85)

Grease and line an 18 cm (7 in) square tin. Sieve flour, baking powder, salt and ginger into a bowl and mix in oatmeal. Rub in butter till the mixture resembles fine breadcrumbs then stir in sugar. Heat treacle till warm and runny then stir in egg and half the buttermilk or sour milk. Stir into dry ingredients, adding more buttermilk until the mixture has a soft dropping consistency. Pour into the tin and bake at 180°C (350°F, Gas 4) for 1–1$\frac{1}{4}$ hours till well risen and firm to the touch. Cool in the tin for 15 minutes before turning out onto a wire rack. Store in an airtight container or foil for 2–3 days before use.

SCOTCH SHORTBREAD

125 g (5 oz) plain flour
25 g (1 oz) rice flour or ground
    rice
Pinch of salt
50 g (2 oz) fine sugar
100 g (4 oz) butter, cut into small
    pieces

Sieve flour, rice flour or ground rice and salt into a bowl and mix in the sugar. Add the butter, and rub in till the mixture resembles breadcrumbs, then knead till it binds together. Form into a 21 cm (8–9 in) round on a lightly floured baking sheet (or sandwich tin) and prick all over. Mark into sections and crimp the edge with fingers and thumb. Cook at 160°C (325°F, Gas 3) for about 45 minutes till light brown. Re-mark sections, sprinkle with fine sugar and leave to cool on the baking sheet. Store in an airtight container.

HIGHLAND SHORTBREAD

200 g (8 oz) plain flour
100 g (4 oz) cornflour (corn-
    starch)
100 g (4 oz) icing (confectioner's)
    sugar
200 g (8 oz) butter, cut into small
    pieces
Fine sugar

Sieve flours and icing sugar into a bowl. Add butter and rub in till mixture resembles breadcrumbs, then knead together to give a stiff dough. Divide into 4 and form into rounds about 5 mm ($\frac{1}{4}$ in) thick on lightly floured baking sheets. Prick all over and mark into sections with a sharp knife. Crimp edges with fingers and thumb and cook at 160°F (325°F, Gas 3) for about 35–40 minutes till pale brown. Re-mark into sections, sprinkle with fine sugar and leave to cool on the baking sheet. Store in an airtight container.

HOGMONAY SHORTBREAD

200 g (8 oz) butter, cut into small
    pieces
75 g (3 oz) fine sugar
150 g (6 oz) plain flour
100 g (4 oz) self-raising flour
50 g (2 oz) ground rice or rice
    flour

Cream butter and sugar till pale, light and fluffy. Sieve flours and ground rice or rice flour together and gradually work into the creamed mixture to give a very smooth paste. Press evenly into two greased sandwich tins and crimp the edges. Prick well and cook at 180°C (350°F, Gas 4) for about 40 minutes till pale brown. Cut into sections while hot then leave to cool in the tins for about 30 minutes before turning out. Remove and store in an airtight container.

PITCAITHLY BANNOCK

200 g (8 oz) plain flour
140 g (5½ oz) butter or margarine,
    cut into small pieces
75 g (3 oz) fine sugar
40 g (1½ oz) mixed chopped peel
25 g (1 oz) blanched almonds,
    chopped

Sieve flour into a bowl, add butter or margarine and rub well into the flour to make a smooth dough. Knead in sugar followed by peel and almonds. Press into a flat round 10–20 mm (½–¾ in) thick on a floured baking sheet and prick all over. Crimp the edges, cover with a piece of greaseproof paper and cook at 180°C (350°F, Gas 4) for 45–50 minutes. Mark into sections, cool on the baking sheet then store in an airtight container.

FLORENTINES

90 g (3½ oz) butter
100 g (4 oz) fine sugar
100 g (4 oz) blanched almonds,
    chopped
25 g (1 oz) sultanas (white raisins)
    chopped
1 tablespoon single (light) cream
25 g (1 oz) glacé cherries,
    chopped
25 g (1 oz) mixed chopped peel
Plain chocolate

Line several baking sheets with greaseproof paper and brush lightly with oil. Melt butter in a pan, add sugar and boil for 1 minute. Add all the other ingredients except the chocolate, mix well and leave to get almost cold. Put small well-shaped heaps of mixture well apart on the greaseproof paper and cook at 180°C (350°F, Gas 4) for about 10 minutes till golden brown. Cool slightly on baking sheets and press the edges with a knife to neaten. Carefully remove to a wire rack with a palette knife and leave to get cold. Melt chocolate in a basin over hot water and spread onto the undersides of biscuits. As the chocolate begins to set mark in wavy lines with a fork. Leave to harden and serve. Makes 20–24.

Note: The biscuits can be stored, without the chocolate coating, in an airtight container separated by sheets of non-stick or waxed paper.

PETTICOAT TAILS

There is doubt about the origin of the name 'Petticoat tails'. Some say it comes from the French *petites Gatelles*, while others say that the name comes from the resemblance of the cakes to the shape of the petticoats worn in the eighteenth century.

150 g (6 oz) plain flour
1 teaspoon caraway seeds
40 g (1½ oz) fine sugar
75 g (3 oz) butter
2 tablespoons milk

Sieve flour into a bowl and add caraway seeds and sugar. Melt butter in a pan with the milk then pour into a well in the centre of the dry ingredients. Mix till well blended and knead lightly (overkneading will spoil the texture). Roll out thinly to a round about 22 cm (9 in) in diameter on a piece of greaseproof paper. Place on a baking sheet. Cut a 7 cm (3 in) circle out of the middle of the round, then cut the outer ring into 8 segments (the 'petticoat tails'). Cook at 180°C (350°F, Gas 4) for 25–30 minutes until firm and lightly browned. Dust with fine sugar, cool on a wire rack, and serve reassembled in the round with the small cut-out circle in the centre and the petticoat tails radiating from it.

PANJOTTERY

'Panjottery' is my family's name for what has inevitably been called 'flea cemeteries'.

200 g (8 oz) shortcrust pastry
(see p. 97)
50 g (2 oz) currants
150 g (6 oz) sultanas (white raisins)
50 g (2 oz) soft brown sugar
50 g (2 oz) mixed peel
200–400 g (½–1 lb) cooking apples, peeled, cored, and chopped
Grated rind of ½ lemon
Beaten egg for glaze

Roll out two-thirds of the pastry and use to line a shallow 19–20 cm (7½–8 in) square tin. Combine currants, sultanas, sugar, peel, apples and lemon rind and place in the pastry-lined tin. Roll out remaining pastry and cut into 10 narrow strips long enough to lay over the top of the tin. Arrange in a lattice pattern over the filling. Dampen ends and stick to the pastry. Trim edges and crimp, then brush with beaten egg. Cook at 220°C (425°F, Gas 7) for 15 minutes then reduce to 180°C (350°F, Gas 4) for about 30 minutes. Serve hot or cold. Serves 6–8.

ABERNETHY BISCUITS

200 g (8 oz) plain flour
Pinch of salt
1 teaspoon baking powder
75 g (3 oz) fine sugar
75 g (3 oz) butter or margarine,
   cut into small pieces
1 egg, beaten
Approx 1 tablespoon milk

Sieve flour, salt and baking powder into a bowl and add sugar. Rub in butter or margarine till the mixture resembles fine breadcrumbs. Add egg and sufficient milk to mix to a stiff paste. Knead lightly and roll out thinly on a floured surface. Cut into 8 cm (3 in) rounds and place on greased baking sheets. Prick well and cook at 180°C (350°F, Gas 4) for about 20 minutes till crisp and golden brown. Cool on a wire rack then store in an airtight container. Makes approx 18.

BRANDY SNAPS

50 g (2 oz) golden syrup
50 g (2 oz) fine sugar
50 g (2 oz) blended lard (shortening)
50 g (2 oz) plain flour
¼ teaspoon ground ginger

Melt golden syrup, sugar and fat in a saucepan and heat gently. Remove from the heat and stir in sieved flour and ginger. Put teaspoons of the mixture onto a well-greased baking sheet keeping spoonsful well apart. Cook at 165°C (325°F, Gas 3) for 8–10 minutes till golden brown. Cool for a few minutes till snaps can be easily removed from baking sheet with a palette knife. Wind round greased spurtles or wooden spoon handles, cool on rack, then slide off the handles when cold. Store in an airtight tin separated by greaseproof or non-stick paper. Serve as they are or filled with whipped cream. Makes approx 18.

Note: If the snaps get too firm to roll easily, put them back in the oven for a minute or so to soften.

MELTING MOMENTS

100 g (4 oz) butter
75 g (3 oz) fine sugar
1 egg yolk
Few drops of vanilla or lemon
   essence
125 g (5 oz) self-raising flour
Crushed cornflakes

Cream the butter and sugar till light and fluffy then beat in egg yolk and essence. Work in the flour and mix to a pliable dough. Divide into walnut-sized pieces, wet hands and roll into balls. Roll in cornflakes and place on a lightly greased baking sheet. Cook at 190°C (375°F, Gas 5) for 15–20 minutes. Cool on a wire rack and when cold store in an airtight container. Makes approx 25.

BASIC PASTRY RECIPES

Shortcrust Pastry

100 g (4 oz) plain flour
A pinch of salt
25 g (1 oz) lard
25 g (1 oz) margarine
Approx 4 teaspoons cold water

Sieve flour and salt into a bowl, rub in the fats till the mixture resembles fine breadcrumbs, then add sufficient water to mix to a stiff, smooth dough. Knead lightly, cover and put to rest, if possible, in a cool place for at least 10 minutes. When the pastry is required, roll it out evenly on a lightly floured board. Cook for 15-20 minutes at 220°C (425°F, Gas 7).

Note: This pastry may be wrapped in polythene and kept in the refrigerator for a day or two before rolling out.

Puff Pastry

200 g (8 oz) plain flour
A pinch of salt
200 g (8 oz) butter (preferably unsalted)
Approx 8 tablespoons cold water
A squeeze of lemon juice
Beaten egg for glazing

Sieve flour and salt. Soften butter with a knife then rub 12 g ($\frac{1}{2}$ oz) into the flour. Mix to an elastic dough with water and lemon juice, knead lightly on a floured board and roll out to a square. Form the remaining butter into an oblong and place to one side of the pastry square. Fold pastry over and seal the edges. With the fold of pastry at the side roll out until the strip is 3 times as long as it is wide. Fold top and bottom in to make 3 thicknesses and seal the edges. Cover the pastry with greaseproof paper and put in a cool place to rest for 20 minutes. Repeat this rolling, folding and resting sequence 5 times more. After the final resting, roll out the pastry as required, brushing the top surface with beaten egg to give the traditional glaze. Cook for 10 minutes at 230°C (450°F, Gas 8).

GLACÉ ICING

100 g (4 oz) icing (confectioner's)
  sugar
Few drops of flavouring essence
  (optional)
1–2 tablespoons warm water

Sieve icing sugar into a bowl and add the flavouring essence if required. Gradually add the warm water, and beat well. The icing should be thick enough to coat the back of a spoon, so if necessary add a little more warm water or sieved icing sugar to obtain the correct consistency. Add colouring, if required, and use at once.

Variations

Orange: Use strained orange juice in place of water.
Lemon: Use strained lemon juice in place of water.
Coffee: Add 1 teaspoon coffee essence and sufficient water to give the required consistency, or dissolve 2 teaspoons instant coffee powder in the water.
Chocolate: Dissolve 2 teaspoons sieved cocoa powder in a little hot water and use with sufficient water to give the required consistency.
Liqueur: Use 2–3 teaspoons chosen liqueur and sufficient water to give the required consistency.

PUDDINGS, TOFFEES AND CANDIES

CLOOTIE DUMPLING

A Clootie Dumpling was a must in many families to mark a birthday. Silver threepenny pieces wrapped in greaseproof paper were added and there was great disappointment if one of the family failed to get one on his or her plate. It took the place of a birthday cake baked to mark an occasion in less frugal households. The leftovers were allowed to cool, then sliced and fried next day—what a treat!

100 g (4 oz) self-raising flour
100 g (4 oz) fresh breadcrumbs
100 g (4 oz) shredded suet
1 teaspoon ground cinnamon
$\frac{1}{4}$ teaspoon ground nutmeg
100 g (4 oz) soft brown sugar
100 g (4 oz) currants
100 g (4 oz) sultanas (white raisins)
100 g (4 oz) raisins
1 egg, beaten (optional)
Milk to mix
Fine sugar

Mix together flour, breadcrumbs, suet, cinnamon, nutmeg and sugar then add the dried fruit. Add the egg and sufficient milk to mix to a fairly soft consistency. Dip a clean cloth in boiling water then dredge with flour. Place in a bowl and put the dumpling mixture into the cloth. Gather up the cloth evenly and tie tightly, but leaving room for the dumpling to expand. Stand the dumpling on a plate in the base of a saucepan and cover with boiling water. Boil gently for $2\frac{1}{2}$–3 hours, topping up with more boiling water as necessary to keep the cloth covered. Remove from pan, carefully turn out of the cloth, dredge with fine sugar and serve with hot custard. Serves 6.

EVE'S PUDDING

50 g (2 oz) butter
50 g (2 oz) fine sugar
1 egg, beaten
50 g (2 oz) flour
$\frac{1}{2}$ teaspoon baking powder
275 g (12 oz) apples, pared and sliced
50 g (2 oz) sugar
1 or 2 cloves

Cream the butter and fine sugar together until light in colour and fluffy. Beat in the egg, a little at a time. Sieve together the flour and baking powder and fold into the mixture carefully. Grease a 500 ml (1 pint) fireproof dish. Place half the prepared apples in the dish, add the sugar and cloves and finally the rest of the apples. Spread the sponge mixture over the top of the apples, covering them completely. Place the dish on a baking tray and put into a pre-heated oven, 190°C (375°F, Gas 5) on the middle shelf. Bake until the sponge is firm and lightly browned (approx $\frac{3}{4}$–1 hour).

99

GRANNY'S PUDDING

100 g (4 oz) fresh breadcrumbs
100 g (4 oz) raisins (stoned or
    seedless)
100 g (4 oz) currants
1 large cooking apple, peeled,
    cored and chopped
100 g (4 oz) soft brown sugar or
    demerara sugar
1 teaspoon ground ginger
½ teaspoon ground nutmeg
3 eggs, beaten
2 tablespoons brandy
4 tablespoons milk

Mix all the ingredients together, binding with the eggs, brandy and milk. Pour into a well greased pudding basin, leaving 2.5 cm (1 in) at the top, and cover first with oiled greaseproof paper then foil or a pudding cloth. Steam or boil for 2½ hours. Turn out and serve with a sweet white cornflour (cornstarch) sauce flavoured with brandy, or a thin custard. Serves 6.

STEWED RHUBARB

400 g (1 lb) rhubarb
85 ml (3 fl oz) water
4 tablespoons sugar
Pinch of ground ginger or 1 tea-
    spoon lemon juice

Cut the leaves off the rhubarb and trim the ends of the stalks. Wash well. Cut into pieces approx 3 cm (1–1½ in) long. Put water, sugar, and ginger or lemon juice on to boil, and when boiling add the rhubarb. Cook gently with the lid on till tender—about 10–15 minutes. Allow to cool.

SCOTCH TRIFLE

1 18 cm (7 in) sponge cake
Raspberry or apricot jam
375 g (15 oz) can grapefruit seg-
    ments, apricot halves, or sliced
    peaches
1 lemon or orange jelly (jello)
4 teaspoons sherry
375 ml (¾ pint) custard
Double (heavy) cream, whipped

Split sponge cake in half and spread liberally with jam. Cut into small pieces and place in the base of a glass dish. Drain fruit and make juice up to 375 ml (¾ pint) with water. Lay the fruit over the sponge. Dissolve jelly in one quarter of the liquid then add the rest of it with the sherry. Pour over fruit and cake and chill till set. Make up custard and pour over the jelly and chill till set. Before serving decorate with whipped cream and any of the following: angelica, glacé cherries, toasted almonds, walnut halves, ratafias, hundreds and thousands. Serves 4–6.

CASTLE TRIFLE

2 18 cm (7 in) sponge cakes
Approx 200 g (½ lb) jam—raspberry, strawberry, apricot etc
250 ml (½ pint) Madeira
4 tablespoons sherry
Approx 700 ml (1–1½ pints) custard
50 g (2 oz) blanched almonds,
  toasted
Ratafia biscuits
Double (heavy) cream, whipped

Divide each cake in half to give four thin layers. Place one in a dish and sprinkle with about a third of the Madeira and sherry. Then spread with a third of the jam and cover with the next sponge layer. Continue to layer up with cake, alcohol and jam, finishing with a plain layer of cake. Cover with the custard and decorate with almonds, ratafias and whipped cream. Chill and serve. Serves 6–8.

SHIVERING TAM

1 lemon
3 large juicy oranges
250 ml (½ pint) cold water
12 g (½ oz) powdered gelatine
Approx 70 g (2–3 oz) fine sugar
Double (heavy) cream, whipped

Grate the rind finely from the lemon and oranges and place in a pan with half the water. Bring to the boil, strain, then dissolve the gelatine in the liquor. Stir in sugar till it melts then make up to just over 250 ml (½ pint) with cold water. Squeeze juice from lemon and oranges, making up to 125 ml (¼ pint) with water if necessary, and strain into the liquor. Pour into a wetted mould and leave to set. Turn out and decorate with whipped cream.

Note: A shivering tam can also be made using any packet of table jelly (jello) made up according to the directions on the packet. Fresh or canned fruit can be added to the jelly before it sets.

ATHOLE BROSE SURPRISE

250 ml (½ pint) double (heavy)
  cream
125 ml (¼ pint) single (light)
  cream
4–8 tablespoons Athole Brose
  (see p. 114)
1–2 egg whites
Little toasted oatmeal or chopped
  walnuts

Combine creams and whisk till thick and almost stiff then whisk in about half the Athole Brose. Whisk egg white till stiff and fold into mixture. Place ½–1 table-spoon Athole Brose in the base of 4–6 glasses and top with the cream. Decorate with toasted oatmeal or walnuts and serve chilled.

DRAMBUIE MERINGUE

15–18 cm (6–7 in) round sponge
   cake (vanilla or chocolate)
2–4 tablespoons Drambuie
275 g (11 oz) can mandarins,
   raspberries or strawberries, etc
Family-sized block of vanilla ice-
   cream
3 egg whites
100 g (4–5 oz) fine sugar

Place the sponge cake on a flat heatproof dish and sprinkle Drambuie all over it. Also spoon a little of the fruit juice over the cake to just moisten. Place ice-cream in the centre of the cake and arrange drained fruit over and around it. Whisk egg whites till stiff then whisk in half the sugar. Fold in remaining sugar and pile meringue all over the whole thing to cover fruit, ice-cream and cake. Cook at 230°C (450°F, Gas 8) for about 3 minutes or until the outside of the meringue begins to brown. Serve immediately. Serves 6.

Note: Prepare and soak sponge before the meal then quickly assemble and cook between courses as this sweet must be taken straight from the oven to the table.

DRAMBUIE CREAM

3 eggs, separated
100 g (4 oz) fine sugar
250 ml (9 fl oz) warm milk
4 teaspoons powdered gelatine
2 tablespoons water
2 tablespoons Drambuie
125 ml (¼ pint) double (heavy)
   cream
2 tablespoons top of the milk
Little whipped cream
Ratafia biscuits
Fresh raspberries (optional)

Beat egg yolks and sugar together till thick then whisk in the milk. Place in the top of a double saucepan and cook over gently simmering water till the mixture thickens sufficiently to coat the back of a spoon. (This cannot be hurried or the custard will curdle.) Dissolve gelatine in the water in a basin over hot water and cool slightly. Whisk into the custard with the Drambuie and chill the mixture till it resembles unbeaten egg white. Whisk cream and milk till very thick but not stiff and fold into the mixture. Finally whisk egg whites till very stiff and fold into the cream mixture. Turn into a lightly greased 1 litre (2 pint) fluted mould and decorate with whipped cream, ratafia biscuits and, if available, fresh raspberries. Serves 6.

Note: A small miniature Drambuie contains 2 tablespoons, the larger miniature 4 tablespoons.

GROSSET MOULD

'Grosset' is a Scots word for gooseberry. There are many gooseberry bushes throughout Scotland—the climate seems to suit them.

400 g (1 lb) gooseberries (fresh or frozen)
2–3 sprays elderflower (optional)
Bare 125 ml ($\frac{1}{4}$ pint) water
Approx 100 g (3–6 oz) sugar
Approx 6 very thin slices brown bread

Top and tail gooseberries and place in a saucepan with the washed elderflowers and water. Cover and simmer gently for about 10 minutes till the fruit is just bursting and soft. Remove flowers and add sugar to taste. Remove crusts from the bread and line a basin with it. Fill up with fruit and most of the juice then cover with remaining bread and juice and then with a weighted plate. Chill for several hours, preferably overnight. Turn out and decorate with whipped double (heavy) cream or serve with pouring single (light) cream. Serves 4–5.

Note: Fresh gooseberries and elderflowers appear at the same time. At other times of the year, when using frozen fruit, replace elderflowers with a sliced orange.

YERNED MILK (Curds and Whey)

500 ml (1 pint) milk
1–2 tablespoons fine sugar
1 teaspoon rennet (or according to directions on the bottle)
Flavourings (see below)

Warm the milk to just blood heat and stir in the sugar until dissolved. Add rennet and pour at once into a bowl or individual dishes. Leave in a warm place to set then chill before serving. Serves 3–4.

Flavourings

Sprinkle a little ground or grated nutmeg on the surface of the mixture before it sets.
Add 1–2 teaspoons rum or brandy to the milk with the sugar.
Add a few drops of almond, vanilla, raspberry, etc, essence to the milk with a little artificial colouring if desired.

TOFFEE AND CANDY

In Scotland, sweetshops are everywhere—sweet sherry sells to a far greater extent than in other parts of Great Britain, and a 'sweetie tin' is to be found in most homes.

Toffee and candy making was a regular winter evening occupation for the very young, courting couples and farm servants in pre-television days. On one Banffshire farm, one night a week was set aside for candy making. It was called 'plunkie night' and the candy was made from the molasses kept in the farm steading for the cattle (it was used in the cattle feed or mash). The recipe used was similar to the following one for treacle candy. Much of the fun came from pulling the candy; if there was a metal coat hook on the door this was used to advantage by well-muscled young men.

TREACLE CANDY

This old-fashioned country candy is still made in this way today—it well repays the effort involved.

1 teaspoon olive oil
2 kg (4 lb) black treacle
2 teaspoons vinegar
Few drops of peppermint, almond or lemon essence
½ teaspoon bicarbonate of soda (baking soda)
½ teaspoon butter to grease hands (optional)

Grease a marble slab or any cool, non-porous surface with oil. In a large, solid-based saucepan mix the treacle and vinegar. Bring to the boil very slowly, stirring frequently to prevent burning. After 20 minutes, test by dropping a little of the mixture into cold water—if it snaps it is cooked. Add the essence, then the soda, and stir very hard for 3 minutes. Remove from the heat and carefully pour the mixture onto the cold slab. Allow to cool. When cool enough to handle, grease hands then pull and twist the mixture till it is light-coloured and tender ('pullin' the candy'). This is most easily done between two people; alternatively use a clean, oiled coat hook fixed at a convenient height on the kitchen wall—pull the mixture into a 'rope', throw it onto the hook, then as the mixture falls, pull the ends and gather them up and throw back on the hook again. Repeat till the mixture is elastic and shiny. Form it into a 45 cm (18 in) length, then cut into 2 cm (¾ in) lengths with well oiled scissors. Let the pieces cool completely, then wrap them in greaseproof or waxed paper and store in an airtight container.

HELENSBURGH TOFFEE

1 kg (2 lb) loaf or granulated
  sugar
1 medium tin condensed milk
100 g (4 oz) salt butter
125 ml (¼ pint) water
1 teaspoon vanilla essence

Put into a heavy pan the sugar, condensed milk, butter and water. Stir frequently over a low heat for 45 minutes. Remove from heat, add vanilla essence and beat well. Pour into a buttered tin and, when cool, cut into squares.

TABLET

4 tablespoons milk
50 g (2 oz) butter
400 g (1 lb) granulated sugar
2 teaspoons golden syrup
1 small can condensed milk
Flavourings (see below)

Grease a 20 cm (8 in) square tin. Put milk and butter into a pan and heat till butter melts. Add sugar and syrup and allow to dissolve slowly. Pour in condensed milk, stirring all the time, and bring to the boil. Boil till 120°C (240°F) is reached, stirring gently. (This is soft ball stage—to test, place a small piece in cold water and roll between the fingers; it should feel like putty when ready.) Beat in chosen flavouring and continue to beat till thick and becoming granular. Pour into the tin and when almost set mark into squares or bars. When cold, cut up and wrap in waxed paper.

Flavourings

The following variations can be used:
Approx ½ teaspoon vanilla essence; 100 g (4 oz) finely chopped walnuts; 2 teaspoons cocoa; 50 g (2 oz) chopped crystallized ginger; 2 tablespoons coffee essence; few drops peppermint essence; finely grated rind of 1 lemon or orange.

BUTTERSCOTCH

400 g (1 lb) soft brown sugar
100 g (4 oz) softened butter
Juice of 1 lemon

Dissolve the sugar very slowly in a heavy saucepan over a gentle heat until liquid. Add butter and lemon juice and boil gently for about 10–15 minutes or until mixture hardens when a little is dropped into cold water. Beat well for about 5 minutes until fairly thick then pour onto a well greased slab or baking sheet. When cool mark into squares by tapping hard and wrap in waxed paper.

JAMS AND JELLIES

Jams and 'jeelies' have always been important to the sweet-toothed Scot. Wild raspberries, brambles (blackberries), rowans and rosehips are there for the taking; whole families and communities go to favourite spots to pick raspberries, and when travelling by train (when trains were more in evidence in Scotland than they are today) it was quite common for the mother to ask the ticket clerk for tickets 'to the rasps'. He would know where they were going.

Scottish raspberries are probably the best in the world, particularly the wild ones in Morayshire and Banffshire along Speyside, where, it has been said, the long, cool summer evenings help the fruit to ripen by slow degrees, each hour enhancing the wonderful flavour. In high summer, daylight often lingers till midnight. Especially round Blairgowrie (an area of Perthshire), the cultivated raspberries are beyond compare, while, all over Scotland, domestic gardens produce in abundance blackcurrants, gooseberries, strawberries, and the more humble but ever-popular rhubarb.

The 'piece-and-jam' or 'jeely piece' was, and still is, the equivalent of the Liverpool 'jam butty'. Living through the hard times of years ago, many a child relied on the 'piece-and-jam' to augment an otherwise rather frugal diet.

'Gies a Piece'

Fin ye skailed frae the school faur ye wirna much eese,
An' ye cleared the aul' dyke wi' a loup,
An' yer mither had cloarted wi' jeely a piece
Forbye it wis only the doup.
Fin ye'd hosed intae that till ye'd brummelled yer lugs
Fit fell off wis licked clean by the cat.
Ye cared nae a docken for basses or rugs,
Wis there onythin' better than that?

William George Cowie

PRESERVING

Here are a few hints to help you on your way to successful jam and jelly making.

1. Fruit used should be sound (preferably just picked), and just ripe—at this stage the pectin content is at its highest.

2. There are two main ways of testing for a set. The most accurate is to use a sugar thermometer. Stir jam thoroughly, put in the thermometer and, when it reaches 105°C (221°F) a set should be obtained. The more common method is to use a saucer. Pour a little jam onto a cold saucer and when cool push a finger across the top of the jam—the surface should wrinkle.

3. A good way to prevent scum on top of the jam is to add a knob of butter and stir till dissolved.

4. All jars used must be scrupulously clean and dry and *warmed* before being filled. Cold jars will crack immediately and ruin the preserve. As soon as a set is reached, fill jars to the necks with jam. (However, strawberry jam and most marmalades are better left to cool for 15 minutes before potting to prevent the fruit rising in the jars.)

5. Wipe the rim and outside of the jar carefully, cover surface of the jam with wax discs, waxed side down (to give a seal), then cover with a dampened cellophane circle held in place with a rubber band. The cover when dry will become taut and airtight. Label jar carefully and store in a cool, dry, and preferably dark place.

6. In jelly making, the fruit should drip untouched through a jelly bag or double thickness of a previously scalded fine cloth (e.g. muslin, tea-towel, pillowcase, etc) for several hours, preferably overnight. Don't poke or squeeze the bag or the finished jelly will be cloudy.

7. Usually the extracted juice should be brought to the boil before adding sugar, for the longer the juice and sugar heat together the darker the jelly becomes and this may spoil the appearance. However, the colour of pale jellies will be improved by the longer heating when sugar is added to the cold juice.

ORANGE MARMALADE

There are many stories claiming that marmalade originated in Scotland, but most are so vague and ridiculous it's best to ignore them. However, there may be some truth in the idea that only the Scots would have used the skin of the orange, which would have been thrown away by less frugal people. There are also many recipes for marmalade—this is a very good one, if not the best.

1.25 kg (3 lb) Seville oranges
Juice of 2 large lemons or 1 teaspoon citric or tartaric acid
3 litres (6 pints) water
2.5 kg (6 lb) sugar

Wash the fruit carefully, halve, and squeeze out the juice and pips. Tie the pips and any fibrous membrane in a muslin bag and place in a preserving pan with the orange and lemon juice (or citric or tartaric acid) and water. Either coarsely mince (grind) or finely slice the peel and add to the pan. Simmer gently for 1½–2 hours till peel is tender and contents of pan reduced by about half. Remove muslin bag, squeezing well, then add sugar and stir till dissolved. Boil rapidly till setting point is reached, leave to stand for 15 minutes then pot and cover in the usual way.

DARK THICK MARMALADE

1.25 kg (3 lb) Seville oranges
3 lemons
3.5 litres (7 pints) water
2.5 kg (6 lb) sugar
2–4 tablespoons black treacle
Whisky (optional)

Wash fruit carefully, halve, and squeeze out the juice and pips. Tie pips and any fibrous membrane in a muslin bag and place in a preserving pan with fruit juices and water. Slice the peel coarsely, add to the pan and simmer gently till the peel is very tender and contents reduced by at least half to give a thick consistency. Add sugar and treacle, and stir till dissolved, then boil rapidly until marmalade is dark and thick and setting point is reached. Cool for 15 minutes then, if liked, stir in 1 tablespoon whisky to each 400 g (1 lb) marmalade. Pot and cover in the usual way.

GRAPEFRUIT MARMALADE

1.25 kg (3 lb) grapefruit
300 g (¾ lb) lemons
3 litres (6 pints) water
2.5 kg (6 lb) sugar

Wipe the fruit, halve, squeeze out the juice and pips. Tie the pips in a muslin bag with any fibrous membrane and put with the juice into a preserving pan. Cut the peel up finely or mince coarsely and add to the pan with the water. Boil for about 2 hours till the peel is tender and the contents of the pan reduced by about half. Remove bag of pips, squeezing well, and add the sugar. Stir till dissolved then boil rapidly till setting point is reached. Cool for 15 minutes then pot and cover in the usual way.

MINT JELLY

2.5 kg (6 lb) cooking apples,
  unpeeled and roughly chopped
1.25 litres (2¼ pints) water
Large bunch of fresh mint
1.25 litres (2¼ pints) vinegar
  (white distilled)
Sugar
6–8 tablespoons freshly chopped
  mint
Green colouring (optional)

Place the apples, water and bunch of mint in a pan and simmer till really soft and mushy. Add vinegar and boil for 5 minutes. Strain through a jelly bag or cloth overnight. Measure juice and return to a clean pan and bring to the boil. Add 400 g (1 lb) of sugar per 500 ml (pint) of juice and stir till sugar has dissolved. Boil rapidly till setting point is reached, stir in chopped mint and a few drops of colouring, if liked, and cool for 15 minutes. Skim, pot and cover in the usual way, preferably in small jars.

ROWAN JELLY

1.75 kg (4 lb) firm ripe rowan
  berries
750 ml (1½ pints) water
4 tablespoons lemon juice
Sugar

Remove berries from the stems and wash thoroughly. Place in a preserving pan with the water and lemon juice. Bring to the boil and simmer for about 1 hour to extract the juice. Strain through a jelly bag or cloth overnight. Measure juice and return to a clean pan and bring to the boil. Add 400 g (1 lb) of sugar to each 500 ml (pint) of juice and stir till dissolved. Boil rapidly till setting point is reached then skim, pot and cover in the usual way.

Note: This jelly has a bitter tang which complements game, venison and fatty meats.

REDCURRANT JELLY

1.25 kg (3 lb) redcurrants
500 ml (1 pint) water
Sugar

Wash fruit thoroughly but do not destalk. Place in a pan with the water and simmer very gently till really soft and broken up. Strain through a jelly bag or cloth overnight. Measure juice and place in a clean pan. Bring to the boil, add 400 g (1 lb) of sugar per 500 ml (pint) of juice and stir till dissolved. Boil rapidly till setting point is reached then skim, pot and cover in the usual way.

Note: As redcurrants are sometimes difficult to come by, the result will be just as satisfactory using frozen fruit.

BRAMBLE JELLY (BLACKBERRY AND APPLE)

1.75 kg (4 lb) brambles (blackberries)
800 g (2 lb) cooking apples, unpeeled and roughly chopped
1 litre (2 pints) water
Sugar

Wash blackberries, place in a pan with the apples and water and simmer till tender. Mash well, and strain through a jelly bag or cloth overnight. Measure juice, place in a clean pan and bring to the boil. Add 400 g (1 lb) of sugar per 500 ml (pint) of juice and stir until dissolved. Boil rapidly till setting point is reached then skim, pot and cover in the usual way.

ROSEHIP AND APPLE JELLY

This jelly is a beautiful colour and has a most delicate flavour.

800 g (2 lb) ripe rosehips
1.5 litres (3 pints) water
800 g (2 lb) cooking apples,
 peeled, cored and roughly
 chopped
700 g (1¾ lb) sugar

Wash the hips thoroughly then place in a pan with the water. Bring to the boil and simmer gently until soft and mushy. Mash the fruit then strain through a jelly bag or cloth overnight. Cook apples slowly in a pan in the minimum of water till mushy, then add the rosehip juice and sugar. Stir till the sugar has dissolved then boil rapidly till setting point is reached. Pot and cover in the usual way.

BLACKCURRANT JAM

1.75 kg (4 lb) blackcurrants
1.5 litres (3 pints) water
2.5 kg (6 lb) sugar

Remove all stems and wash if necessary. Place black-currants in a preserving pan with the water and simmer till fruit is tender and the contents of the pan well reduced, stirring occasionally to prevent the fruit sticking. Add the sugar, stir till dissolved then boil rapidly till setting point is reached. Pot and cover in the usual way.

UNCOOKED RASPBERRY (RASPS) JAM

400 g (1 lb) sugar
400 g (1 lb) hulled raspberries

Warm the sugar in a bowl either in the oven or on top of it. Mash the raspberries and add to the warmed sugar. Stir continuously until the sugar has dissolved. Pot and cover in the usual way. This jam thickens with keeping and has an excellent flavour.

Note: The fruit used for this recipe must be perfect, dry and freshly picked for good results.

Butterscotch (p. 105), Helensburgh Toffee (p. 105), Tablet (p. 105) and Treacle Candy (p. 104).

Preserves (pp. 108-112).

RASPBERRY (RASPS) JAM

1.75 kg (4 lb) hulled raspberries
1.75 kg (4 lb) sugar

Wash fruit and simmer very gently in its own juice for 15–20 minutes till really tender. Add the sugar and stir till dissolved then boil rapidly till setting point is reached. Pot and cover in the usual way.

GOOSEBERRY JAM

2 kg (4½ lb) gooseberries
750 ml (1½ pints) water
2.75 kg (6 lb) sugar

Top, tail and wash gooseberries and place in a preserving pan with the water. Simmer gently for about 30 minutes till the fruit is really soft and well reduced, stirring occasionally to prevent sticking. Add the sugar, stir till dissolved, then boil rapidly till setting point is reached. Pot and cover in the usual way.

Note: The degree of colour of the jam depends on the variety and maturity of the fruit used. Prolonged boiling with the sugar gives a deeper colour and boiling in a brass or copper pan gives a greener colour. For a variation on the flavour add 12–16 heads of elderflowers tied in muslin and cook with the gooseberries. Remove before adding the sugar.

RHUBARB AND GINGER JAM

Rhubarb is grown extensively in Scottish gardens and in some parts in the south is even cultivated in the field for sale in the greengrocers and for the jam making and canning companies. The largest rhubarb field in the world is reputed to be in Riddrie, a suburb of Glasgow.

1.25 kg (3 lb) prepared rhubarb
1.25 kg (3 lb) sugar
Juice of 3 lemons
25 g (1 oz) root ginger, bruised
Approx 85 g (2–4 oz) preserved
   or crystallized ginger, chopped

Wipe rhubarb and cut into chunks about 2 cm (1 in) long. Put in a large bowl in layers with the sugar. Add lemon juice and leave to stand overnight. Place in a pan with the bruised ginger tied in muslin and bring to the boil. Boil rapidly for 15–20 minutes then remove muslin bag. Add chopped ginger and reboil for 5 minutes, or until the rhubarb is clear and setting point is reached. Pot and cover in the usual way.

Note: Delicious served with milk puddings and vanilla-flavoured cream and blancmanges.

111

Highland malt whiskies.

Scottish store cupboard.

LEMON CURD

4 eggs, beaten
Grated rind and juice of 4 lemons
100 g (4 oz) butter
400 g (1 lb) sugar

Place all the ingredients in the top of a double saucepan or in a basin over a pan of gently simmering water. Stir continously till the sugar dissolves, then continue heating till the curd thickens, stirring occasionally. Strain carefully into small sterilized jars and cover in the usual way. Store in a cool place and use within 3–4 weeks.

DRINKS

There's the wonderful love of a beautiful maid
And the love of a staunch true man,
And the love of a baby that's unafraid—
They've been there since time began.

But the most wonderful love—the love of loves—
Even greater than that of a mother,
Is the tender, infinite, passionate love
Of one pie-eyed drunk for another.

Anon

'Drink is a terrible thing!' How often one hears this said in Scotland, the home of Scotch whisky, which is what this section of the book is all about. The Kirk and teetotallers may denounce it, but the fact is good whisky is one of man's best friends, if treated with respect.

WHAT IS MALT WHISKY?

Until the middle of the last century, the whisky drunk in Scotland and England was, to all intents and purposes, pure Highland malt, produced on Speyside, in the counties of Banffshire and Morayshire, and other distilleries throughout Scotland whose names are now immortalized on the bottles: Glenfarclas, Glenlivet, Glenfiddich, Glen Grant, Mortlach, Strahisla, Highland Park, Glenmorangie, Laphroaig, and many more.

Then there was a move by south of Scotland businessmen to promote the sale of a patent still or grain whisky, which had the advantage of simplicity of manufacture – like gin or similar spirits, it could be turned out almost by factory methods. But the resulting alcohol had little taste to recommend it, so to add character it was blended with a number of malt whiskies from the Highland distilleries. It had been said that the Highland malts were too strong for sedentary town dwellers, and the new blended whiskies were sold in the south and elsewhere on this dubious claim; however, while blending became the general practice, a small quantity of straight malt whisky was always retained by the Highland distilleries and bottled and sold locally. Possibly as a result of the increased number of tourists visiting Scotland and drinking the local malts, there has grown up an interest in and demand for these delightful, individual whiskies, with their haunting Highland names. A great number of them are now being exported all over the world.

No visit to the north of Scotland is complete without a visit to a Highland distillery and an invitation to sample a 'wee drappie o' the cratur'. (Why whisky should be called this is not known to me, unless the Scots considered it to be foremost among their 'creature' comforts.) Each malt distillery produces its own distinctive whisky; the spring water used in the production varies from glen to glen, and has the same effect on the whisky as the growing conditions in a French vineyard affect the nature of a chateau-bottled wine. Added to this, the malt whisky is matured in casks for years in the pure, cool, damp Highland air, giving a unique character to each distillery's spirit.

While we hesitate to tamper with anything as perfect as whisky, whether malt or blended, the following recipes are some of the traditional variations, and well worth trying on the right occasion.

ATHOLE BROSE

This recipe appeared in a cookery book printed for private circulation by the 8th Duke of Atholl (1871–1942), but there is no record of when Athole Brose was originally made at Blair Castle in Perthshire.

4 tablespoons runny honey
4 sherry glasses medium oatmeal
Whisky

Use heather honey if you can get it. Apart from its unique flavour, it is one honey that remains runny and never crystallizes. To prepare the oatmeal, put it into a basin and mix with cold water to the consistency of a thick paste. Pass the oatmeal through a fine strainer, taking care not to make it too watery. Stir the honey and oatmeal well together and put into a litre (2 pint) bottle. Fill up with whisky. Shake well before serving.

TODDY

There are various methods of making toddy, but this is the method used by the old Highland farmer whose recipe for porridge has also been used in this book. Some faint-hearts add lemon juice, but he never did — 'Na, na, dina spile good whisky!'

Loaf or granulated sugar
Hot water
Whisky (any blended whisky will do, but a Highland malt whisky will give a better toddy)

Fill the glasses or tumblers in which the toddy is to be served with hot water to warm, and empty them. Place 2 or 3 lumps of loaf sugar, or 2 or 3 teaspoons of granulated sugar, in the bottom of the warmed glasses. Add sufficient hot water to dissolve the sugar (a sherry glassful should be enough). Add the same amount of whisky and stir. Add the same amount of hot water and stir again. Add the same amount of whisky, stir, and drink.

RUSTY NAIL

To two-thirds Drambuie add one-third Highland malt whisky, and serve. This is also known as 'A Knuckle-head' or 'An Edinburgh'.

AN OLD HIGHLAND LIQUEUR

200 g (½ lb) raisins
6 g (¼ oz) each of nutmeg, cloves
  and cardamoms
Rind of a Seville orange
Few drops of tincture of saffron
100 g (¼ lb) brown candy sugar
  (or barley sugar)
1 litre (2 pints) whisky, malt or
  blended

Chop or mince (grind) the raisins. Bruise the nutmeg, cloves and cardamoms in a mortar. Rub the orange rind against a lump of sugar, and put the resulting juice in a large bottle. Add the tincture of saffron and the candy sugar or barley sugar. Cover with whisky, and cork. Shake every day for a fortnight. Filter, bottle and cork. Serve in liqueur glasses. (This is a Meg Dods recipe.)

WHAT IS A DRAM?

To be invited to have a dram or drammie is an indication that your host is offering you a glass of whisky, the size of the dram depending on his generosity — though originally it was one-third of a gill (nearly 50 ml).

> When neebors anger at a plea,
> An' just as wud as wud can be,
> How easy can the barley-bree
> Cement the quarrel!
> It's aye the cheapest lawyer's fee
> To taste the barrel.
>
> Robert Burns

INDEX

117